Jesus is perhaps the most influential person who has ever lived.

Luke's Gospel is one of the most famous historical accounts of his life.

You may not identify with being religious and you might feel cautious at the idea of reading the Bible.
But the gospel of Luke is written for people like you.

Contents

Turn the page for how to use Uncover Luke.

Introducing **Luke**

Luke's Gospel is a historical record of Jesus' life. In AD 80, Luke, a doctor, collated his account. He did so precisely and methodically. In his introduction, he writes of how he has 'carefully investigated everything from the beginning' by speaking with eyewitnesses who had personally met Jesus.

But as we read his account, what emerges is far more than dry history. Luke masterfully paints a portrait of Jesus.

Extraordinary power, yet radical humility.

Wisdom which confused the wise, yet made sense to little children.

A man whose presence brought joy and healing, yet who chose to walk a path of deepest sorrow and shame.

In Luke's Gospel, we meet countless men and women who are transformed as they encounter Jesus and the kingdom of God he spoke about.

Throughout history, entire cultures have been transformed as Luke's Gospel has inspired many to fight for justice and the cause of the oppressed.

More personally, individuals have found that as they open these pages, they discover a vision of life and an experience of love unlike any other.

However spiritual or sceptical you might be, **Uncover Luke** is an invitation for you to consider Jesus for yourself.

How to use **Uncover Luke**

Option One
Read from the beginning

You could turn to **page 6** and start reading Luke's account from the beginning. Make notes along the way if that helps you.

Throughout Uncover Luke there are moments for you to pause and explore more deeply:

Six studies will help you to uncover six moments in Luke's Gospel. Use them to discuss and process what you are reading with a friend.

Five personal reflections give space for you to pause, look at some artwork, read a section of Luke's account, and reflect on it in your own time.

Option Two
Start at Study One

If you are reading Uncover with a friend, turn to the first study on **page 12** and start reading from there.

In between each study, you could read the intervening chapters and make use of the five personal reflections in your own time.

The Gospel of **Luke**

1 Many have undertaken to draw up an account of the things that have been fulfilled among us, [2] just as they were handed down to us by those who from the first were eyewitnesses and servants of the word. [3] With this in mind, since I myself have carefully investigated everything from the beginning, I too decided to write an orderly account for you, most excellent Theophilus, [4] so that you may know the certainty of the things you have been taught.

The birth of John the Baptist foretold

[5] In the time of Herod king of Judea there was a priest named Zechariah, who belonged to the priestly division of Abijah; his wife Elizabeth was also a descendant of Aaron. [6] Both of them were righteous in the sight of God, observing all the Lord's commands and decrees blamelessly. [7] But they were childless because Elizabeth was not able to conceive, and they were both very old.

[8] Once when Zechariah's division was on duty and he was serving as priest before God, [9] he was chosen by lot, according to the custom of the priesthood, to go into the temple of the Lord and burn incense. [10] And when the time for the burning of incense came, all the assembled worshippers were praying outside.

[11] Then an angel of the Lord appeared to him, standing at the right side of the altar of incense. [12] When Zechariah saw him, he was startled and was gripped with fear. [13] But the angel said to him: 'Do not be afraid, Zechariah; your prayer has been heard. Your wife Elizabeth will bear you a son, and you are to call him John. [14] He will be a joy and delight to you, and many will rejoice because of his birth, [15] for he will be great in the sight of the Lord. He is never to take wine or other fermented drink, and he will be filled with the Holy Spirit even before he is born. [16] He will bring back many of the people of Israel to the Lord their God. [17] And he will go on before the Lord, in the spirit and power of Elijah, to turn the hearts of the parents to their children and the disobedient to the wisdom of the righteous — to make ready a people prepared for the Lord.'

[18] Zechariah asked the angel, 'How can I be sure of this? I am an old man and my wife is well along in years.'

[19] The angel said to him, 'I am Gabriel. I stand in the presence of God, and I have been sent to speak to you and to tell you this good news. [20] And now you will be silent and not able to speak until the day this happens, because you did not believe my words, which will come true at their appointed time.'

²¹ Meanwhile, the people were waiting for Zechariah and wondering why he stayed so long in the temple. ²² When he came out, he could not speak to them. They realised he had seen a vision in the temple, for he kept making signs to them but remained unable to speak.

²³ When his time of service was completed, he returned home.

²⁴ After this his wife Elizabeth became pregnant and for five months remained in seclusion. ²⁵ 'The Lord has done this for me,' she said. 'In these days he has shown his favour and taken away my disgrace among the people.'

The birth of Jesus foretold

²⁶ In the sixth month of Elizabeth's pregnancy, God sent the angel Gabriel to Nazareth, a town in Galilee, ²⁷ to a virgin pledged to be married to a man named Joseph, a descendant of David. The virgin's name was Mary. ²⁸ The angel went to her and said, 'Greetings, you who are highly favoured! The Lord is with you.'

²⁹ Mary was greatly troubled at his words and wondered what kind of greeting this might be. ³⁰ But the angel said to her, 'Do not be afraid, Mary, you have found favour with God. ³¹ You will conceive and give birth to a son, and you are to call him Jesus. ³² He will be great and will be called the Son of the Most High. The Lord God will give him the throne of his father David, ³³ and he will reign over Jacob's descendants forever; his kingdom will never end.'

³⁴ 'How will this be,' Mary asked the angel, 'since I am a virgin?'

³⁵ The angel answered, 'The Holy Spirit will come on you, and the power of the Most High will overshadow you. So the holy one to be born will be called the Son of God. ³⁶ Even Elizabeth your relative is going to have a child in her old age, and she who was said to be unable to conceive is in her sixth month. ³⁷ For no word from God will ever fail.'

³⁸ 'I am the Lord's servant,' Mary answered. 'May your word to me be fulfilled.' Then the angel left her.

Mary visits Elizabeth

³⁹ At that time Mary got ready and hurried to a town in the hill country of Judea, ⁴⁰ where she entered Zechariah's home and greeted Elizabeth. ⁴¹ When Elizabeth heard Mary's greeting, the baby leaped in her womb, and Elizabeth was filled with the Holy Spirit. ⁴² In a loud voice she exclaimed: 'Blessed are you among women, and blessed is the child you will bear! ⁴³ But why am I so favoured, that the mother of my Lord should come to me? ⁴⁴ As soon as the sound of your greeting reached my ears, the baby in my womb leaped for joy. ⁴⁵ Blessed is she who has believed that the Lord would fulfil his promises to her!'

Mary's song

⁴⁶ And Mary said:
'My soul glorifies the Lord
⁴⁷ and my spirit rejoices in God my Saviour,
⁴⁸ for he has been mindful
  of the humble state of his servant.
From now on all generations will call me blessed,
⁴⁹ for the Mighty One has done great things for me —
  holy is his name.
⁵⁰ His mercy extends to those who fear him,
  from generation to generation.
⁵¹ He has performed mighty deeds with his arm;
  he has scattered those who are proud in their inmost thoughts.
⁵² He has brought down rulers from their thrones
  but has lifted up the humble.
⁵³ He has filled the hungry with good things
  but has sent the rich away empty.
⁵⁴ He has helped his servant Israel,
  remembering to be merciful
⁵⁵ to Abraham and his descendants forever,

just as he promised our ancestors.'

⁵⁶ Mary stayed with Elizabeth for about three months and then returned home.

The birth of John the Baptist

⁵⁷ When it was time for Elizabeth to have her baby, she gave birth to a son. ⁵⁸ Her neighbours and relatives heard that the Lord had shown her great mercy, and they shared her joy.

⁵⁹ On the eighth day they came to circumcise the child, and they were going to name him after his father Zechariah, ⁶⁰ but his mother spoke up and said, 'No! He is to be called John.'

⁶¹ They said to her, 'There is no one among your relatives who has that name.'

⁶² Then they made signs to his father, to find out what he would like to name the child. ⁶³ He asked for a writing tablet, and to everyone's astonishment he wrote, 'His name is John.' ⁶⁴ Immediately his mouth was opened and his tongue set free, and he began to speak, praising God. ⁶⁵ All the neighbours were filled with awe, and throughout the hill country of Judea people were talking about all these things.

⁶⁶ Everyone who heard this wondered about it, asking, 'What then is this child going to be?' For the Lord's hand was with him.

Zechariah's song

⁶⁷ His father Zechariah was filled with the Holy Spirit and prophesied:

⁶⁸ 'Praise be to the Lord, the God of Israel,
  because he has come to his people and redeemed them.
⁶⁹ He has raised up a horn of salvation for us
  in the house of his servant David
⁷⁰ (as he said through his holy prophets of long ago),
⁷¹ salvation from our enemies
  and from the hand of all who hate us—

[72] to show mercy to our ancestors

and to remember his holy covenant,

[73] the oath he swore to our father Abraham:

[74] to rescue us from the hand of our enemies,

and to enable us to serve him without fear

[75] in holiness and righteousness before him all our days.

[76] And you, my child, will be called a prophet of the Most High;

for you will go on before the Lord to prepare the way for him,

[77] to give his people the knowledge of salvation

through the forgiveness of their sins,

[78] because of the tender mercy of our God,

by which the rising sun will come to us from heaven

[79] to shine on those living in darkness

and in the shadow of death,

to guide our feet into the path of peace.'

[80] And the child grew and became strong in spirit; and he lived in the wilderness until he appeared publicly to Israel.

Encounter

Study 1

LUKE 2:1-20

In the rhythms of everyday life, it is easy to miss the things that are most important and beautiful.

DISCUSS

1. What do you think prevents us from noticing extraordinary things in our day-to-day lives?

As we start our journey with Luke, we begin with his record of Jesus' birth: the account of the first Christmas.

READ LUKE 2:1-3

Luke is a doctor who wrote an 'orderly account' of Jesus' life by carefully gathering the stories of eyewitnesses.

2.   What do verses 1 - 3 suggest about the kind of account Luke is writing?

Luke is writing real history. His account begins with a young couple named Mary and Joseph.

They are ordinary. Normal people, living in an unimportant town, under Roman rule.

They also face challenges. Mary is not yet married but has been told by an angelic messenger that she will give birth to the Son of God (see Luke 1:35). Being pregnant and unmarried in that culture would have been very shameful. Moreover, the Romans have now imposed a census on the people. Joseph and the heavily pregnant Mary are forced to make a 90-mile journey to Bethlehem.

READ LUKE 2:4-7

Mary is likely one of the eyewitnesses that Luke spoke with.

3.   Look through verses 4 - 7 and imagine you are Mary. How might you be feeling as you travel and then give birth?

The birth of Jesus

2 In those days Caesar Augustus issued a decree that a census should be taken of the entire Roman world. [2] (This was the first census that took place while Quirinius was governor of Syria.)

[3] And everyone went to their own town to register.

[4] So Joseph also went up from the town of Nazareth in Galilee to Judea, to Bethlehem the town of David, because he belonged to the house and line of David. [5] He went there to register with Mary, who was pledged to be married to him and was expecting a child. [6] While they were there, the time came for the baby to be born, [7] and she gave birth to her firstborn, a son. She wrapped him in cloths and placed him in a manger, because there was no guest room available for them.

Census - an official population count, issued by the Romans.
David - a significant king in Israel's history.

Luke draws our attention to a group of shepherds. Shepherds lived on the margins. They were often poor, seen as non-religious, and had a reputation for being thieves. Yet it is to these men, in the dark of night, that a crowd of angels announce the birth of a saviour from God: the birth of Jesus.

Luke was writing to a non-Jewish audience. Talk of angels would have sounded as strange to them as it may do for us. Yet Luke does not shy away from recounting events that were clearly supernatural.

4.   What do the shepherds see and hear? Why do you think they respond in the way they do?

The scope of the angels' announcement is huge. The saviour will bring joy to 'all the people'. Yet the shepherds receive this personal message: he has been born 'to you'.

5.   Consider the kind of people the shepherds were. What does it suggest about God, that he would announce the arrival of his saviour to them before anyone else?

Going about their normal lives, the shepherds encounter a reality bigger than themselves: the arrival of a 'saviour' who will bring widespread joy.

The angels call this saviour 'the Messiah'. It is the name for a promised king that God's people had been waiting for. Their scriptures were full of promises about how this figure would come to rescue and restore them.

⁸ And there were shepherds living out in the fields near by, keeping watch over their flocks at night. ⁹ An angel of the Lord appeared to them, and the glory of the Lord shone around them, and they were terrified. ¹⁰ But the angel said to them, 'Do not be afraid. I bring you good news that will cause great joy for all the people. ¹¹ Today in the town of David a Saviour has been born to you; he is the Messiah, the Lord. ¹² This will be a sign to you: you will find a baby wrapped in cloths and lying in a manger.'

¹³ Suddenly a great company of the heavenly host appeared with the angel, praising God and saying,

¹⁴ 'Glory to God in the highest heaven,

and on earth peace to those on whom his favour rests.'

¹⁵ When the angels had left them and gone into heaven, the shepherds said to one another, 'Let's go to Bethlehem and see this thing that has happened, which the Lord has told us about.'

Heavenly host - a multitude of angels.

One of these promises was written by a prophet called Micah. He spoke of this Messiah coming from the town Mary has just given birth in: Bethlehem.

Read what he says:

² But you, Bethlehem Ephrathah,
  are the smallest town in Judah.
Your family is almost too small to count,
  but the "Ruler of Israel" will come from you to rule for me.
His beginnings are from ancient times,
  from long, long ago.
³ The Lord will let his people be defeated
  until the woman gives birth to her child, the promised king.
Then the rest of his brothers will come back
  to join the people of Israel.
⁴ He will begin to rule Israel in the power of the Lord.
  Like a shepherd, he will lead his people in the wonderful
name of the Lord his God.
And they will live in safety
  because then his greatness will be known all over the world.
⁵ He will bring a time of peace.

Micah 5

(ERV)

6.   **What does Micah say the Messiah will be like?**

7.   **In Luke's account, what will be the 'sign' that the shepherds have found the Messiah? What does this 'sign' suggest about the kind of saviour Jesus might be?**

Jesus is the strong and powerful Messiah. He is 'the Lord' (verse 11), a title given to God himself. Yet he comes as a helpless baby into the mess, dirt, and difficulty of life.

As Jesus the Messiah comes in vulnerability to a broken world, it is 'good news that will cause great joy for all the people'. God has come close to help and to heal his people, a help and healing that we will see as we read through Luke's account.

8.   Why do you think the shepherds are no longer fearful, but joyful?

9.   Imagine you are Mary. The shepherds arrive, sharing the angels' announcement about your new baby. What might you be 'treasuring' and 'pondering'?

> *Just like the shepherds, amid her struggles Mary has encountered a bigger reality. Could it be that this story of hope, joy, and salvation is really coming true?*

[16] So they hurried off and found Mary and Joseph, and the baby, who was lying in the manger. [17] When they had seen him, they spread the word concerning what had been told them about this child, [18] and all who heard it were amazed at what the shepherds said to them. [19] But Mary treasured up all these things and pondered them in her heart. [20] The shepherds returned, glorifying and praising God for all the things they had heard and seen, which were just as they had been told.

[21] On the eighth day, when it was time to circumcise the child, he was named Jesus, the name the angel had given him before he was conceived.

Jesus presented in the temple

[22] When the time came for the purification rites required by the Law of Moses, Joseph and Mary took him to Jerusalem to present him to the Lord [23] (as it is written in the Law of the Lord, 'Every firstborn male is to be consecrated to the Lord'), [24] and to offer a sacrifice in keeping with what is said in the Law of the Lord: 'a pair of doves or two young pigeons.'

Process **together**

Luke ends this section by showing a range of responses to Jesus' birth.

Mary ponders these things. The shepherds erupt in praise. People who hear are amazed. What about you?

10. **What opinions do you have about Jesus? How have you come to those conclusions?**

Mary and the shepherds lived ordinary and often difficult lives. Yet they encounter something extraordinary. Their experiences show them something: they are part of a bigger story. A story of hope and joy. A story centred on Jesus.

Not everyone has experienced angelic revelation. But many people's circumstances have led them to wonder whether this bigger story of hope might be true.

11. **Have your own circumstances ever prompted you to want God to be real?**

Whoever you are, Luke invites you to experience his account of Jesus, and, like Mary, to ponder these things for yourself.

PAUSE

Sit in stillness for a moment.

LOOK

Notice what stands out in the artwork.

READ

Read the passage slowly, once or twice.

REFLECT

Use the questions to guide your
thoughts and response.

²⁵ Now there was a man in Jerusalem called Simeon, who was righteous and devout. He was waiting for the consolation of Israel, and the Holy Spirit was on him. ²⁶ It had been revealed to him by the Holy Spirit that he would not die before he had seen the Lord's Messiah. ²⁷ Moved by the Spirit, he went into the temple courts. When the parents brought in the child Jesus to do for him what the custom of the Law required, ²⁸ Simeon took him in his arms and praised God, saying:

> ²⁹ 'Sovereign Lord, as you have promised,
> you may now dismiss your servant in peace.
> ³⁰ For my eyes have seen your salvation,
> ³¹ which you have prepared in the sight of all nations:
> ³² a light for revelation to the Gentiles,
> and the glory of your people Israel.'

³³ The child's father and mother marvelled at what was said about him. ³⁴ Then Simeon blessed them and said to Mary, his mother: 'This child is destined to cause the falling and rising of many in Israel, and to be a sign that will be spoken against, ³⁵ so that the thoughts of many hearts will be revealed. And a sword will pierce your own soul too.'

³⁶ There was also a prophet, Anna, the daughter of Penuel, of the tribe of Asher. She was very old; she had lived with her husband seven years after her marriage, ³⁷ and then was a widow until she was eighty-four. She never left the temple but worshipped night and day, fasting and praying. ³⁸ Coming up to them at that very moment, she gave thanks to God and spoke about the child to all who were looking forward to the redemption of Jerusalem.

As humans, we struggle. But we also hope.

Simeon's aging body is getting weaker. Decades of grief weigh on Anna's heart.

They have both waited a lifetime for the day God would comfort and rescue humanity. As they hold the young Jesus, they believe that their hopes have been realised.

1.   **What do you think it would feel like to wait your whole life for something, to then finally see it?**

2.   **Listen again to what Simeon and Anna say. What sounds most hopeful to you? What sounds strange?**

3.   **Are there ways that you experience weakness or grief? What is it that you long for? Where do you look for hope?**

Look again at the artwork.
Does anything different stand out to you?

³⁹ When Joseph and Mary had done everything required by the Law of the Lord, they returned to Galilee to their own town of Nazareth. ⁴⁰ And the child grew and became strong; he was filled with wisdom, and the grace of God was on him.

The boy Jesus at the temple

⁴¹ Every year Jesus' parents went to Jerusalem for the Festival of the Passover. ⁴² When he was twelve years old, they went up to the festival, according to the custom. ⁴³ After the festival was over, while his parents were returning home, the boy Jesus stayed behind in Jerusalem, but they were unaware of it. ⁴⁴ Thinking he was in their company, they travelled on for a day. Then they began looking for him among their relatives and friends. ⁴⁵ When they did not find him, they went back to Jerusalem to look for him. ⁴⁶ After three days they found him in the temple courts, sitting among the teachers, listening to them and asking them questions. ⁴⁷ Everyone who heard him was amazed at his understanding and his answers. ⁴⁸ When his parents saw him, they were astonished. His mother said to him, 'Son, why have you treated us like this? Your father and I have been anxiously searching for you.'

⁴⁹ 'Why were you searching for me?' he asked. 'Didn't you know I had to be in my Father's house?' ⁵⁰ But they did not understand what he was saying to them.

⁵¹ Then he went down to Nazareth with them and was obedient to them. But his mother treasured all these things in her heart. ⁵² And Jesus grew in wisdom and stature, and in favour with God and man.

John the Baptist prepares the way

3 In the fifteenth year of the reign of Tiberius Caesar– when Pontius Pilate was governor of Judea, Herod tetrarch of Galilee, his brother Philip tetrarch of Iturea and Traconitis, and Lysanias tetrarch of Abilene - ² during the high-priesthood of Annas and Caiaphas, the word of God came to John son of Zechariah in the wilderness. [3] He went into all the country around the Jordan, preaching a baptism of repentance for the forgiveness of sins. [4] As it is written in the book of the words of Isaiah the prophet:

"A voice of one calling in the wilderness,
"Prepare the way for the Lord,
  make straight paths for him.
[5] Every valley shall be filled in,
  every mountain and hill made low.
The crooked roads shall become straight,
  the rough ways smooth.
[6] And all people will see God's salvation.'"

[7] John said to the crowds coming out to be baptised by him, 'You brood of vipers! Who warned you to flee from the coming wrath?

[8] Produce fruit in keeping with repentance. And do not begin to say to yourselves, "We have Abraham as our father." For I tell you that out of these stones God can raise up children for Abraham. [9] The axe has been laid to the root of the trees, and every tree that does not produce good fruit will be cut down and thrown into the fire.'

[10] 'What should we do then?' the crowd asked.

[11] John answered, 'Anyone who has two shirts should share with the one who has none, and anyone who has food should do the same.'

[12] Even tax collectors came to be baptised. 'Teacher,' they asked, 'what should we do?'

[13] 'Don't collect any more than you are required to,' he told them.

[14] Then some soldiers asked him, 'And what should we do?'

He replied, 'Don't extort money and don't accuse people falsely– be content with your pay.'

[15] The people were waiting expectantly and were all wondering in

their hearts if John might possibly be the Messiah. [16] John answered them all, 'I baptise you with water. But one who is more powerful than I will come, the straps of whose sandals I am not worthy to untie. He will baptise you with the Holy Spirit and fire. [17] His winnowing fork is in his hand to clear his threshing-floor and to gather the wheat into his barn, but he will burn up the chaff with unquenchable fire.' [18] And with many other words John exhorted the people and proclaimed the good news to them.

[19] But when John rebuked Herod the tetrarch because of his marriage to Herodias, his brother's wife, and all the other evil things he had done, [20] Herod added this to them all: he locked John up in prison.

The baptism and genealogy of Jesus

[21] When all the people were being baptised, Jesus was baptised too. And as he was praying, heaven was opened [22] and the Holy Spirit descended on him in bodily form like a dove. And a voice came from heaven: 'You are my Son, whom I love; with you I am well pleased.'

[23] Now Jesus himself was about thirty years old when he began his ministry. He was the son, so it was thought, of Joseph,

the son of Heli, [24] the son of Matthat,
the son of Levi, the son of Melki,
the son of Jannai, the son of Joseph,
[25] the son of Mattathias, the son of Amos,
the son of Nahum, the son of Esli,
the son of Naggai, [26] the son of Maath,
the son of Mattathias, the son of Semein,
the son of Josek, the son of Joda,
[27] the son of Joanan, the son of Rhesa,

the son of Zerubbabel, the son of Shealtiel,
the son of Neri, 28 the son of Melki,
the son of Addi, the son of Cosam,
the son of Elmadam, the son of Er,
29 the son of Joshua, the son of Eliezer,
the son of Jorim, the son of Matthat,
the son of Levi, 30 the son of Simeon,
the son of Judah, the son of Joseph,
the son of Jonam, the son of Eliakim,
31 the son of Melea, the son of Menna,
the son of Mattatha, the son of Nathan,
the son of David, 32 the son of Jesse,
the son of Obed, the son of Boaz,
the son of Salmon, the son of Nahshon,
33 the son of Amminadab, the son of Ram,
the son of Hezron, the son of Perez,
the son of Judah, 34 the son of Jacob,
the son of Isaac, the son of Abraham,
the son of Terah, the son of Nahor,
35 the son of Serug, the son of Reu,
the son of Peleg, the son of Eber,
the son of Shelah, 36 the son of Cainan,
the son of Arphaxad, the son of Shem,
the son of Noah, the son of Lamech,
37 the son of Methuselah, the son of Enoch,
the son of Jared, the son of Mahalalel,
the son of Kenan, 38 the son of Enosh,
the son of Seth, the son of Adam,
the son of God.

Jesus is tested in the wilderness

4 Jesus, full of the Holy Spirit, left the Jordan and was led by the Spirit into the wilderness, [2] where for forty days he was tempted by the devil. He ate nothing during those days, and at the end of them he was hungry.

[3] The devil said to him, 'If you are the Son of God, tell this stone to become bread.' [4] Jesus answered, 'It is written: "Man shall not live on bread alone." '

[5] The devil led him up to a high place and showed him in an instant all the kingdoms of the world. [6] And he said to him, 'I will give you all their authority and splendour; it has been given to me, and I can give it to anyone I want to. [7] If you worship me, it will all be yours.'

[8] Jesus answered, 'It is written: "Worship the Lord your God and

serve him only." [9] The devil led him to Jerusalem and had him stand on the highest point of the temple. 'If you are the Son of God,' he said, 'throw yourself down from here. [10] For it is written:

"'He will command his angels concerning you
    to guard you carefully;
[11] they will lift you up in their hands,
    so that you will not strike your foot against a stone.'"

[12] Jesus answered, 'It is said: "Do not put the Lord your God to the test."'

[13] When the devil had finished all this tempting, he left him until an opportune time.

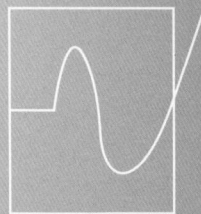

Hope

Study 2

The way we view the future often depends on our general outlook. An optimist sees lots of reasons to hope. By contrast, a pessimist focuses on worst-case scenarios.

1. As you look to the future, do you tend towards optimism or pessimism? Why?

Having described Jesus' birth, in chapters 2 & 3 Luke has given more proof that Jesus is the long-awaited saviour and Messiah. Now we pick up the story as Jesus causes a stir in his hometown of Nazareth.

Jews regularly gathered in the synagogue to hear teaching from their sacred scriptures. As a scroll is handed to Jesus, he reads from a text written by the prophet Isaiah more than 600 years before his birth.

READ LUKE 4:14-19

2.   What are the main themes of the words that Jesus reads?

> *Jesus' listeners are Judeans under Roman occupation. They are an oppressed nation. Suffering from high taxes and limited freedom, they would have felt trapped. Understandably the frustrations of life leave them looking for hope.*
>
> *The Romans were quick to stamp out any threat to their rule. This left little hope of a rebellion. Instead, most people were waiting for the Messiah, a powerful king who would rescue them. The words that Jesus reads speak of this Messiah.*

3.   Imagine yourself as one of Jesus' listeners. As you hear Jesus read Isaiah's words, what do you find most appealing?

4.   Verse 18 refers to those who are 'poor'. How do verses 18-19 help expand our understanding of who the 'poor' might include?'

> *When Jesus uses the word 'poor', he's talking about anyone who is in need. He uses the example of those who are trapped, weak, and excluded. But for anyone who feels their need, Jesus comes with good news: the promise of knowing the help and favour of God.*

Jesus rejected at Nazareth

¹⁴ Jesus returned to Galilee in the power of the Spirit, and news about him spread through the whole countryside. ¹⁵ He was teaching in their synagogues, and everyone praised him. ¹⁶ He went to Nazareth, where he had been brought up, and on the Sabbath day he went into the synagogue, as was his custom. He stood up to read, ¹⁷ and the scroll of the prophet Isaiah was handed to him. Unrolling it, he found the place where it is written:

¹⁸ 'The Spirit of the Lord is on me,
    because he has anointed me
    to proclaim good news to the poor.
He has sent me to proclaim freedom for the prisoners
    and recovery of sight for the blind,
to set the oppressed free,
¹⁹   to proclaim the year of the Lord's favour.'

Sabbath - a weekly God-ordained day of rest.
Isaiah - a Jewish prophet.

Luke tells us that everyone's eyes were fixed on Jesus, wondering what would happen next.

5. **What is Jesus claiming about himself?**

6. **What do you notice about the people's initial response to Jesus' claim?**

On hearing the magnitude of Jesus' claim, his hearers are amazed. But if you read on, their amazement soon turns to doubt and then to hostility.

They are offended when Jesus offers his 'good news' to non-Judean people. But perhaps most crucially, they find it hard to receive Jesus' 'good news' because they do not truly see themselves as poor and needy.

Study continues on page 49

²⁰ Then he rolled up the scroll, gave it back to the attendant and sat down. The eyes of everyone in the synagogue were fastened on him. ²¹ He began by saying to them, 'Today this scripture is fulfilled in your hearing.'

²² All spoke well of him and were amazed at the gracious words that came from his lips. 'Isn't this Joseph's son?' they asked.

²³ Jesus said to them, 'Surely you will quote this proverb to me: "Physician, heal yourself!" And you will tell me, "Do here in your home town what we have heard that you did in Capernaum."'

²⁴ 'Truly I tell you,' he continued, 'no prophet is accepted in his home town. ²⁵ I assure you that there were many widows in Israel in Elijah's time, when the sky was shut for three and a half years and there was a severe famine throughout the land. ²⁶ Yet Elijah was not sent to any of them, but to a widow in Zarephath in the region of Sidon. ²⁷ And there were many in Israel with leprosy in the time of Elisha the prophet, yet not one of them was cleansed - only Naaman the Syrian.'

²⁸ All the people in the synagogue were furious when they heard this.

²⁹ They got up, drove him out of the town, and took him to the brow of the hill on which the town was built, in order to throw him off the cliff. ³⁰ But he walked right through the crowd and went on his way.

Jesus drives out an impure spirit

³¹ Then he went down to Capernaum, a town in Galilee, and on the Sabbath he taught the people. ³² They were amazed at his teaching, because his words had authority.

³³ In the synagogue there was a man possessed by a demon, an impure spirit. He cried out at the top of his voice, ³⁴ 'Go away! What do you want with us, Jesus of Nazareth? Have you come to destroy us? I know who you are - the Holy One of God!'

³⁵ 'Be quiet!' Jesus said sternly. 'Come out of him!' Then the demon threw the man down before them all and came out without injuring him.

³⁶ All the people were amazed and said to each other, 'What words these are! With authority and power he gives orders to impure spirits and they come out!' ³⁷ And the news about him spread throughout the surrounding area.

Jesus heals many

³⁸ Jesus left the synagogue and went to the home of Simon. Now Simon's mother-in-law was suffering from a high fever, and they asked Jesus to help her. ³⁹ So he bent over her and rebuked the fever, and it left her. She got up at once and began to wait on them.

⁴⁰ At sunset, the people brought to Jesus all who had various kinds of illness, and laying his hands on each one, he healed them. ⁴¹ Moreover, demons came out of many people, shouting, 'You are the Son of God!' But he rebuked them and would not allow them to speak, because they knew he was the Messiah.

⁴² At daybreak, Jesus went out to a solitary place. The people were looking for him and when they came to where he was, they tried to keep him from leaving them. ⁴³ But he said, 'I must proclaim the good news of the kingdom of God to the other towns also, because that is why I was sent.' ⁴⁴ And he kept on preaching in the synagogues of Judea.

Jesus calls his first disciples

5 One day as Jesus was standing by the Lake of Gennesaret, the people were crowding around him and listening to the word of God. ² He saw at the water's edge two boats, left there by the fishermen, who were washing their nets. ³ He got into one of the boats, the one belonging to Simon, and asked him to put out a little from shore. Then he sat down and taught the people from the boat.

⁴ When he had finished speaking, he said to Simon, 'Put out into deep water, and let down the nets for a catch.' ⁵ Simon answered, 'Master, we've worked hard all night and haven't caught anything. But because you say so, I will let down the nets.' ⁶ When they had done so, they caught such a large number of fish that their nets began to break. ⁷ So they signalled their partners in the other boat to come and help them, and they came and filled both boats so full that they began to sink. ⁸ When Simon Peter saw this, he fell at Jesus'

knees and said, 'Go away from me, Lord; I am a sinful man!' [9] For he and all his companions were astonished at the catch of fish they had taken, [10] and so were James and John, the sons of Zebedee, Simon's partners. Then Jesus said to Simon, 'Don't be afraid; from now on you will fish for people.' [11] So they pulled their boats up on shore, left everything and followed him.

Jesus heals a man with leprosy

[12] While Jesus was in one of the towns, a man came along who was covered with leprosy. When he saw Jesus, he fell with his face to the ground and begged him, 'Lord, if you are willing, you can make me clean.' [13] Jesus reached out his hand and touched the man. 'I am willing,' he said. 'Be clean!' And immediately the leprosy left him.

[14] Then Jesus ordered him, 'Don't tell anyone, but go, show yourself to the priest and offer the sacrifices that Moses commanded for your cleansing, as a testimony to them.' [15] Yet the news about him spread all the more, so that crowds of people came to hear him and to be healed of their illnesses. [16] But Jesus often withdrew to lonely places and prayed.

Jesus forgives and heals a paralysed man

[17] One day Jesus was teaching, and Pharisees and teachers of the law were sitting there. They had come from every village of Galilee and from Judea and Jerusalem. And the power of the Lord was with Jesus to heal those who were ill. [18] Some men came carrying a paralysed man on a mat and tried to take him into the house to lay him before Jesus. [19] When they could not find a way to do this because of the crowd, they went up on the roof and lowered him on his mat through the tiles into the middle of the crowd, right in front of Jesus.

[20] When Jesus saw their faith, he said, 'Friend, your sins are forgiven.'

²¹ The Pharisees and the teachers of the law began thinking to themselves, 'Who is this fellow who speaks blasphemy? Who can forgive sins but God alone?'

²² Jesus knew what they were thinking and asked, 'Why are you thinking these things in your hearts? ²³ Which is easier: to say, "Your sins are forgiven," or to say, "Get up and walk"? ²⁴ But I want you to know that the Son of Man has authority on earth to forgive sins.' So he said to the paralysed man, 'I tell you, get up, take your mat and go home.' ²⁵ Immediately he stood up in front of them, took what he had been lying on and went home praising God. ²⁶ Everyone was amazed and gave praise to God. They were filled with awe and said, 'We have seen remarkable things today.'

Jesus calls Levi and eats with sinners

²⁷ After this, Jesus went out and saw a tax collector by the name of Levi sitting at his tax booth. 'Follow me,' Jesus said to him, ²⁸ and Levi got up, left everything and followed him.

²⁹ Then Levi held a great banquet for Jesus at his house, and a large crowd of tax collectors and others were eating with them.

³⁰ But the Pharisees and the teachers of the law who belonged to their sect complained to his disciples, 'Why do you eat and drink with tax collectors and sinners?'

³¹ Jesus answered them, 'It is not the healthy who need a doctor, but those who are ill. ³² I have not come to call the righteous, but sinners to repentance.'

Jesus questioned about fasting

³³ They said to him, 'John's disciples often fast and pray, and so do the disciples of the Pharisees, but yours go on eating and drinking.'

³⁴ Jesus answered, 'Can you make the friends of the bridegroom fast while he is with them? ³⁵ But the time will come when the bridegroom will be taken from them; in those days they will fast.'

³⁶ He told them this parable: 'No one tears a piece out of a new garment to patch an old one. Otherwise, they will have torn the new garment, and the patch from the new will not match the old. ³⁷ And no one pours new wine into old wineskins. Otherwise, the new wine will burst the skins; the wine will run out and the wineskins will be ruined. ³⁸ No, new wine must be poured into new wineskins. ³⁹ And no one after drinking old wine wants the new, for they say, "The old is better."'

Jesus is Lord of the Sabbath

6 One Sabbath Jesus was going through the cornfields, and his disciples began to pick some ears of corn, rub them in their hands and eat the grain. ² Some of the Pharisees asked, 'Why are you doing what is unlawful on the Sabbath?'

³ Jesus answered them, 'Have you never read what David did when he and his companions were hungry? ⁴ He entered the house of God, and taking the consecrated bread, he ate what is lawful only for priests to eat. And he also gave some to his companions.' ⁵ Then Jesus said to them, 'The Son of Man is Lord of the Sabbath.'

⁶ On another Sabbath he went into the synagogue and was teaching, and a man was there whose right hand was shrivelled.

⁷ The Pharisees and the teachers of the law were looking for a reason to accuse Jesus, so they watched him closely to see if he would heal on the Sabbath. ⁸ But Jesus knew what they were thinking and said to the man with the shrivelled hand, 'Get up and stand in front of everyone.' So he got up and stood there.

⁹ Then Jesus said to them, 'I ask you, which is lawful on the Sabbath: to do good or to do evil, to save life or to destroy it?'

¹⁰ He looked around at them all, and then said to the man, 'Stretch out your hand.' He did so, and his hand was completely restored. ¹¹ But the Pharisees and the teachers of the law were furious and began to discuss with one another what they might do to Jesus.

The twelve apostles

¹² One of those days Jesus went out to a mountainside to pray, and spent the night praying to God. ¹³ When morning came, he called his disciples to him and chose twelve of them, whom he also designated apostles: ¹⁴ Simon (whom he named Peter), his brother Andrew, James, John, Philip, Bartholomew, ¹⁵ Matthew, Thomas, James son of Alphaeus, Simon who was called the Zealot, ¹⁶ Judas son of James, and Judas Iscariot, who became a traitor.

Blessings and woes

¹⁷ He went down with them and stood on a level place. A large crowd of his disciples was there and a great number of people from all over Judea, from Jerusalem, and from the coastal region around Tyre and Sidon, ¹⁸ who had come to hear him and to be healed of their diseases. Those troubled by impure spirits were cured, ¹⁹ and the people all tried to touch him, because power was coming from him and healing them all.

²⁰ Looking at his disciples, he said:
'Blessed are you who are poor,
for yours is the kingdom of God.
²¹ Blessed are you who hunger now,
for you will be satisfied.
Blessed are you who weep now,
for you will laugh.
²² Blessed are you when people hate you,
when they exclude you and insult you
and reject your name as evil,
because of the Son of Man.
²³ 'Rejoice in that day and leap for joy, because great is your reward in heaven. For that is how their ancestors treated the prophets.

²⁴ 'But woe to you who are rich,
    for you have already received your comfort.
²⁵ Woe to you who are well fed now,
    for you will go hungry.
Woe to you who laugh now,
    for you will mourn and weep.
²⁶ Woe to you when everyone speaks well of you,
    for that is how their ancestors treated the false prophets.

Love for enemies

²⁷ 'But to you who are listening I say: Love your enemies, do good to those who hate you, ²⁸ bless those who curse you, pray for those who mistreat you. ²⁹ If someone slaps you on one cheek, turn to them the other also. If someone takes your coat, do not withhold your shirt from them. ³⁰ Give to everyone who asks you, and if anyone takes what belongs to you, do not demand it back. ³¹ Do to others as you would have them do to you.

³² 'If you love those who love you, what credit is that to you? Even sinners love those who love them. ³³ And if you do good to those who are good to you, what credit is that to you? Even sinners do that. ³⁴ And if you lend to those from whom you expect repayment, what credit is that to you? Even sinners lend to sinners, expecting to be repaid in full. ³⁵ But love your enemies, do good to them, and lend to them without expecting to get anything back. Then your reward will be great, and you will be children of the Most High, because he is kind to the ungrateful and wicked. ³⁶ Be merciful, just as your Father is merciful.

Judging others

³⁷ 'Do not judge, and you will not be judged. Do not condemn, and you will not be condemned. Forgive, and you will be forgiven. ³⁸ Give,

and it will be given to you. A good measure, pressed down, shaken together and running over, will be poured into your lap. For with the measure you use, it will be measured to you.'

³⁹ He also told them this parable: 'Can the blind lead the blind? Will they not both fall into a pit? ⁴⁰ The student is not above the teacher, but everyone who is fully trained will be like their teacher.

⁴¹ 'Why do you look at the speck of sawdust in your brother's eye and pay no attention to the plank in your own eye? ⁴² How can you say to your brother, "Brother, let me take the speck out of your eye," when you yourself fail to see the plank in your own eye? You hypocrite, first take the plank out of your eye, and then you will see clearly to remove the speck from your brother's eye.

A tree and its fruit

⁴³ 'No good tree bears bad fruit, nor does a bad tree bear good fruit. ⁴⁴ Each tree is recognised by its own fruit. People do not pick figs from thorn bushes, or grapes from briers. ⁴⁵ A good man brings good things out of the good stored up in his heart, and an evil man brings evil things out of the evil stored up in his heart. For the mouth speaks what the heart is full of.

The wise and foolish builders

⁴⁶ 'Why do you call me, "Lord, Lord," and do not do what I say? ⁴⁷ As for everyone who comes to me and hears my words and puts them into practice, I will show you what they are like. ⁴⁸ They are like a man building a house, who dug down deep and laid the foundation on rock. When a flood came, the torrent struck that house but could not shake it, because it was well built. ⁴⁹ But the one who hears my words and does not put them into practice is like a man who built a house on the ground without a foundation. The moment the torrent struck that house, it collapsed and its destruction was complete.'

The faith of the centurion

7 When Jesus had finished saying all this to the people who were listening, he entered Capernaum. ² There a centurion's servant, whom his master valued highly, was ill and about to die.

³ The centurion heard of Jesus and sent some elders of the Jews to him, asking him to come and heal his servant. ⁴ When they came to Jesus, they pleaded earnestly with him, 'This man deserves to have you do this, ⁵ because he loves our nation and has built our synagogue.' ⁶ So Jesus went with them.

He was not far from the house when the centurion sent friends to say to him: 'Lord, don't trouble yourself, for I do not deserve to have you come under my roof. ⁷ That is why I did not even consider myself worthy to come to you. But say the word, and my servant will be healed. ⁸ For I myself am a man under authority, with soldiers under me. I tell this one, "Go," and he goes; and that one, "Come," and he comes. I say to my servant, "Do this," and he does it.'

⁹ When Jesus heard this, he was amazed at him, and turning to the crowd following him, he said, 'I tell you, I have not found such great faith even in Israel.' ¹⁰ Then the men who had been sent returned to the house and found the servant well.

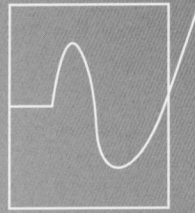

Hope

Study 2

Study 2
Continuing from page 39

For those who do consider themselves poor and needy, meeting Jesus is transformative. We see this play out as Jesus meets a widow.

READ LUKE 7:11-17

Two crowds meet at the edge of the town: one with Jesus, one carrying a dead man to bury him outside of the city.

7. **What would have been the different moods in these two crowds?**

8. **How does Luke's description of the funeral show it to be particularly hopeless?**

As the widow mourns the loss of her son, it no doubt reawakens the pain of losing her husband. In a culture where men held the economic power, she is left alone and vulnerable.

The widow does not ask for help, but as Jesus sees her, he chooses to act.

9. **Read verse 13. What do you think motivates Jesus to respond in the way he does to this hopeless situation?**

Touching a coffin would have made someone ceremonially unclean in the eyes of the community. But Jesus stops the procession as he deliberately walks through the crowd to place his hand on the coffin.

10. **What do verses 14 - 15 show us about how Jesus delivers 'good news to the poor'?**

This woman cannot offer Jesus anything. Yet without being asked, Jesus tenderly steps in to restore her son to life. As Jesus gives back the boy to his mother, he does so as a gift. Jesus always acts like this.

He offers help and healing to people as a gift, not as something they have to earn.

11. **Consider the crowd's response to Jesus' miracle. What hope do they now express?**

Jesus raises a widow's son

11 Soon afterwards, Jesus went to a town called Nain, and his disciples and a large crowd went along with him. 12 As he approached the town gate, a dead person was being carried out - the only son of his mother, and she was a widow. And a large crowd from the town was with her. 13 When the Lord saw her, his heart went out to her and he said, 'Don't cry.'

14 Then he went up and touched the bier they were carrying him on, and the bearers stood still. He said, 'Young man, I say to you, get up!' 15 The dead man sat up and began to talk, and Jesus gave him back to his mother.

16 They were all filled with awe and praised God. 'A great prophet has appeared among us,' they said. 'God has come to help his people.' 17 This news about Jesus spread throughout Judea and the surrounding country.

Bier - a frame for carrying the dead.

Process **together**

In the face of human hopelessness and helplessness, Jesus is moved to compassion. But his compassion is not merely a feeling. It moves him to action. And as he raises the dead son, he shows that he has the power to turn hopeless situations around.

Jesus' actions verify his claim to bring 'good news to the poor.' As we continue to read Luke's Gospel, we will continue to see Jesus freeing people from their sickness, their past, and their shame. These people all realise that they can't help themselves.. They realise that they are 'poor.'

The crowds in Nazareth struggle to accept Jesus' claims because they struggle to see themselves as 'poor.' They aren't prepared to see themselves as hopeless.

12. **What might keep us from seeing ourselves as needy?**

13. **Where do you turn for hope as you look to the future?**

Jesus and John the Baptist

¹⁸ John's disciples told him about all these things. Calling two of them, ¹⁹ he sent them to the Lord to ask, 'Are you the one who is to come, or should we expect someone else?'

²⁰ When the men came to Jesus, they said, 'John the Baptist sent us to you to ask, "Are you the one who is to come, or should we expect someone else?"' ²¹ At that very time Jesus cured many who had diseases, illnesses and evil spirits, and gave sight to many who were blind. ²² So he replied to the messengers, 'Go back and report to John what you have seen and heard: the blind receive sight, the lame walk, those who have leprosy are cleansed, the deaf hear, the dead are raised, and the good news is proclaimed to the poor. ²³ Blessed is anyone who does not stumble on account of me.' ²⁴ After John's messengers left, Jesus began to speak to the crowd about John: 'What did you go out into the wilderness to see? A reed swayed by the wind? ²⁵ If not, what did you go out to see? A man dressed in fine clothes? No, those who wear expensive clothes and indulge in luxury are in palaces. ²⁶ But what did you go out to see? A prophet? Yes, I tell you, and more than a prophet. ²⁷ This is the one about whom it is written:

"'I will send my messenger ahead of you,
    who will prepare your way before you."

²⁸ I tell you, among those born of women there is no one greater than John; yet the one who is least in the kingdom of God is greater than he.'

²⁹ (All the people, even the tax collectors, when they heard Jesus' words, acknowledged that God's way was right, because they had been baptised by John. ³⁰ But the Pharisees and the experts in the law rejected God's purpose for themselves, because they had not been baptised by John.)

[31] Jesus went on to say, 'To what, then, can I compare the people of this generation? What are they like? [32] They are like children sitting in the market-place and calling out to each other:

"We played the pipe for you,
  and you did not dance;
we sang a dirge,
  and you did not cry."

[33] For John the Baptist came neither eating bread nor drinking wine, and you say, "He has a demon." [34] The Son of Man came eating and drinking, and you say, "Here is a glutton and a drunkard, a friend of tax collectors and sinners." [35] But wisdom is proved right by all her children.'

PERSONAL REFLECTION

PAUSE
Sit in stillness for a moment.

LOOK
Notice what stands out in the artwork.

READ
Read the passage slowly, once or twice.

REFLECT
Use the questions to guide your
thoughts and response.

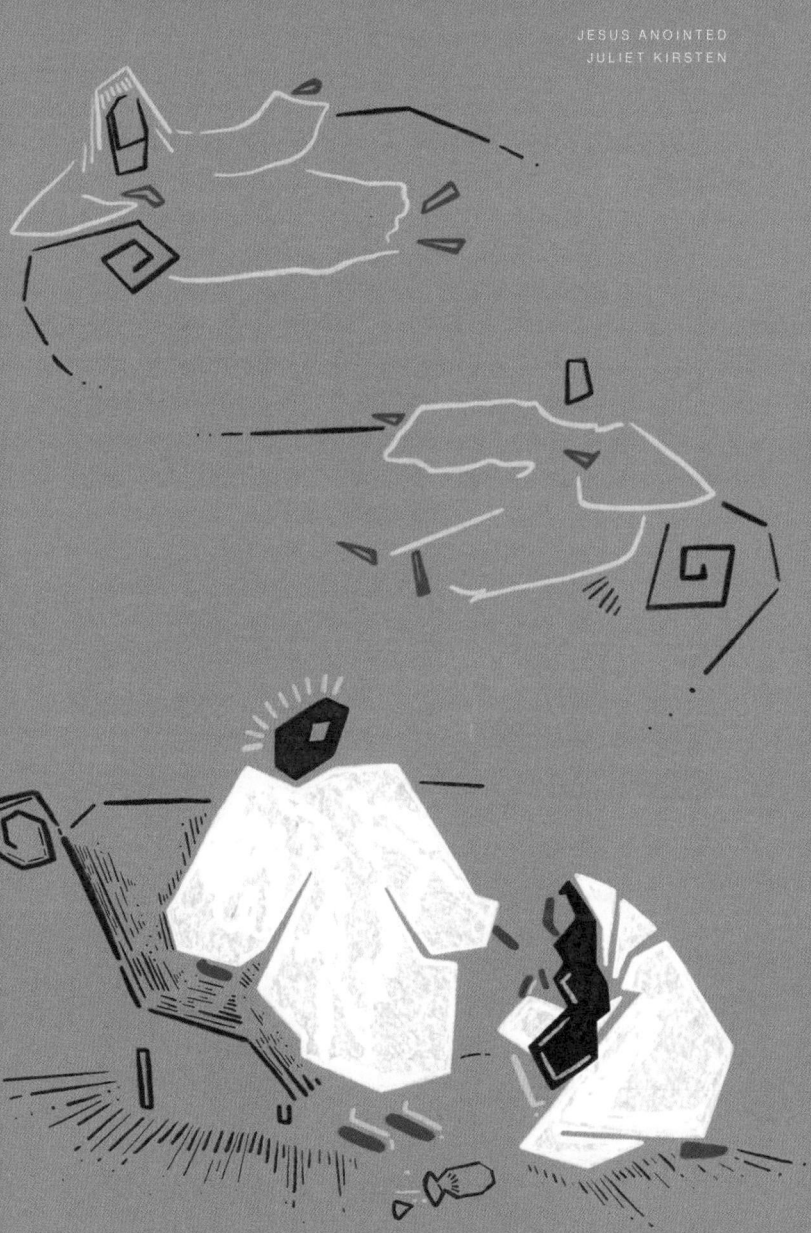

57

Jesus anointed by a sinful woman

[36] When one of the Pharisees invited Jesus to have dinner with him, he went to the Pharisee's house and reclined at the table. [37] A woman in that town who lived a sinful life learned that Jesus was eating at the Pharisee's house, so she came there with an alabaster jar of perfume. [38] As she stood behind him at his feet weeping, she began to wet his feet with her tears. Then she wiped them with her hair, kissed them and poured perfume on them.

[39] When the Pharisee who had invited him saw this, he said to himself, 'If this man were a prophet, he would know who is touching him and what kind of woman she is - that she is a sinner.'

[40] Jesus answered him, 'Simon, I have something to tell you.'

'Tell me, teacher,' he said.

[41] 'Two people owed money to a certain money-lender. One owed him five hundred denarii, and the other fifty. [42] Neither of them had the money to pay him back, so he forgave the debts of both. Now which of them will love him more?'

[43] Simon replied, 'I suppose the one who had the bigger debt forgiven.'

'You have judged correctly,' Jesus said.

[44] Then he turned toward the woman and said to Simon, 'Do you see this woman? I came into your house. You did not give me any water for my feet, but she wet my feet with her tears and wiped them with her hair. [45] You did not give me a kiss, but this woman, from the time I entered, has not stopped kissing my feet. [46] You did not put oil on my head, but she has poured perfume on my feet. [47] Therefore, I tell you, her many sins have been forgiven - as her great love has shown. But whoever has been forgiven little loves little.'

[48] Then Jesus said to her, 'Your sins are forgiven.'

[49] The other guests began to say among themselves, 'Who is this who even forgives sins?'

[50] Jesus said to the woman, 'Your faith has saved you; go in peace.'

Jesus is invited to a dinner with the wealthy and important.

Yet our attention is drawn to a woman who was known for her life of immorality. She was probably a prostitute. We do not even know her name.

Her presence is unwelcome and her outpouring of love draws attention.

1. **Why do you think Simon is so offended by Jesus' welcome of this woman?**

2. **What does Jesus want Simon to understand about love?**

3. **Imagine you are this woman. Listen to what Jesus says about you. Listen to what he says *to* you. How do you feel?**

Look again at the artwork.
Does anything different stand out to you?

The parable of the sower

8 After this, Jesus travelled about from one town and village to another, proclaiming the good news of the kingdom of God. The Twelve were with him, ² and also some women who had been cured of evil spirits and diseases: Mary (called Magdalene) from whom seven demons had come out; ³ Joanna the wife of Chuza, the manager of Herod's household; Susanna; and many others. These women were helping to support them out of their own means.

⁴ While a large crowd was gathering and people were coming to Jesus from town after town, he told this parable: ⁵ 'A farmer went out to sow his seed. As he was scattering the seed, some fell along the path; it was trampled on, and the birds ate it up. ⁶ Some fell on rocky ground, and when it came up, the plants withered because they had no moisture. ⁷ Other seed fell among thorns, which grew up with it and choked the plants. ⁸ Still other seed fell on good soil. It came up and yielded a crop, a hundred times more than was sown.'

When he said this, he called out, 'Whoever has ears to hear, let them hear.'

⁹ His disciples asked him what this parable meant. ¹⁰ He said, 'The knowledge of the secrets of the kingdom of God has been given to you, but to others I speak in parables, so that,

"though seeing, they may not see;
though hearing, they may not understand."

¹¹ 'This is the meaning of the parable: The seed is the word of God. ¹² Those along the path are the ones who hear, and then the devil comes and takes away the word from their hearts, so that they may not believe and be saved. ¹³ Those on the rocky ground are the ones who receive the word with joy when they hear it, but they have no root. They believe for a while, but in the time of testing they fall away. ¹⁴ The seed that fell among thorns stands for those who hear,

but as they go on their way they are choked by life's worries, riches and pleasures, and they do not mature. [15] But the seed on good soil stands for those with a noble and good heart, who hear the word, retain it, and by persevering produce a crop.

A lamp on a stand

[16] 'No one lights a lamp and hides it in a clay jar or puts it under a bed. Instead, they put it on a stand, so that those who come in can see the light. [17] For there is nothing hidden that will not be disclosed, and nothing concealed that will not be known or brought out into the open. [18] Therefore consider carefully how you listen. Whoever has will be given more; whoever does not have, even what they think they have will be taken from them.'

Jesus' mother and brothers

[19] Now Jesus' mother and brothers came to see him, but they were not able to get near him because of the crowd. [20] Someone told him, 'Your mother and brothers are standing outside, wanting to see you.'

[21] He replied, 'My mother and brothers are those who hear God's word and put it into practice.'

Jesus calms the storm

[22] One day Jesus said to his disciples, 'Let us go over to the other side of the lake.' So they got into a boat and set out. [23] As they sailed, he fell asleep. A squall came down on the lake, so that the boat was being swamped, and they were in great danger.

[24] The disciples went and woke him, saying, 'Master, Master, we're going to drown!'

He got up and rebuked the wind and the raging waters; the storm subsided, and all was calm. [25] 'Where is your faith?' he asked his disciples.

In fear and amazement they asked one another, 'Who is this? He commands even the winds and the water, and they obey him.'

Jesus restores a demon-possessed man

²⁶ They sailed to the region of the Gerasenes, which is across the lake from Galilee. ²⁷ When Jesus stepped ashore, he was met by a demon-possessed man from the town. For a long time this man had not worn clothes or lived in a house, but had lived in the tombs. ²⁸ When he saw Jesus, he cried out and fell at his feet, shouting at the top of his voice, 'What do you want with me, Jesus, Son of the Most High God? I beg you, don't torture me!' ²⁹ For Jesus had commanded the impure spirit to come out of the man. Many times it had seized him, and though he was chained hand and foot and kept under guard, he had broken his chains and had been driven by the demon into solitary places.

³⁰ Jesus asked him, 'What is your name?'

'Legion,' he replied, because many demons had gone into him.

³¹ And they begged Jesus repeatedly not to order them to go into the Abyss.

³² A large herd of pigs was feeding there on the hillside. The demons begged Jesus to let them go into the pigs, and he gave them permission. ³³ When the demons came out of the man, they went into the pigs, and the herd rushed down the steep bank into the lake and was drowned.

³⁴ When those tending the pigs saw what had happened, they ran off and reported this in the town and countryside, ³⁵ and the people went out to see what had happened. When they came to Jesus, they found the man from whom the demons had gone out, sitting at Jesus' feet, dressed and in his right mind; and they were afraid. ³⁶ Those who had seen it told the people how the demon-possessed man had been cured. ³⁷ Then all the people of the region of the Gerasenes asked Jesus to leave them, because they were overcome with fear.

So he got into the boat and left.

⁳⁸ The man from whom the demons had gone out begged to go with him, but Jesus sent him away, saying, ³⁹ 'Return home and tell how much God has done for you.' So the man went away and told all over town how much Jesus had done for him.

Jesus raises a dead girl and heals a sick woman

⁴⁰ Now when Jesus returned, a crowd welcomed him, for they were all expecting him. ⁴¹ Then a man named Jairus, a synagogue leader, came and fell at Jesus' feet, pleading with him to come to his house ⁴² because his only daughter, a girl of about twelve, was dying.

As Jesus was on his way, the crowds almost crushed him. ⁴³ And a woman was there who had been subject to bleeding for twelve years, but no one could heal her. ⁴⁴ She came up behind him and touched the edge of his cloak, and immediately her bleeding stopped.

⁴⁵ 'Who touched me?' Jesus asked.

When they all denied it, Peter said, 'Master, the people are crowding and pressing against you.'

⁴⁶ But Jesus said, 'Someone touched me; I know that power has gone out from me.'

⁴⁷ Then the woman, seeing that she could not go unnoticed, came trembling and fell at his feet. In the presence of all the people, she told why she had touched him and how she had been instantly healed.

⁴⁸ Then he said to her, 'Daughter, your faith has healed you. Go in peace.'

⁴⁹ While Jesus was still speaking, someone came from the house of Jairus, the synagogue leader. 'Your daughter is dead,' he said. 'Don't bother the teacher anymore.'

⁵⁰ Hearing this, Jesus said to Jairus, 'Don't be afraid; just believe, and she will be healed.'

⁵¹ When he arrived at the house of Jairus, he did not let anyone go

in with him except Peter, John and James, and the child's father and mother. [52] Meanwhile, all the people were wailing and mourning for her. 'Stop wailing,' Jesus said. 'She is not dead but asleep.'

[53] They laughed at him, knowing that she was dead. [54] But he took her by the hand and said, 'My child, get up!' [55] Her spirit returned, and at once she stood up. Then Jesus told them to give her something to eat. [56] Her parents were astonished, but he ordered them not to tell anyone what had happened.

Jesus sends out the Twelve

9 When Jesus had called the Twelve together, he gave them power and authority to drive out all demons and to cure diseases, [2] and he sent them out to proclaim the kingdom of God and to heal those who were ill. [3] He told them: 'Take nothing for the journey - no staff, no bag, no bread, no money, no extra shirt.

[4] Whatever house you enter, stay there until you leave that town.

[5] If people do not welcome you, leave their town and shake the dust off your feet as a testimony against them.' [6] So they set out and went from village to village, proclaiming the good news and healing people everywhere.

[7] Now Herod the tetrarch heard about all that was going on. And he was perplexed because some were saying that John had been raised from the dead, [8] others that Elijah had appeared, and still others that one of the prophets of long ago had come back to life. [9] But Herod said, 'I beheaded John. Who, then, is this I hear such things about?' And he tried to see him.

Jesus feeds the five thousand

[10] When the apostles returned, they reported to Jesus what they had done. Then he took them with him and they withdrew by themselves to a town called Bethsaida, [11] but the crowds learned about it and followed him. He welcomed them and spoke to them

about the kingdom of God, and healed those who needed healing.

¹² Late in the afternoon the Twelve came to him and said, 'Send the crowd away so they can go to the surrounding villages and countryside and find food and lodging, because we are in a remote place here.'

¹³ He replied, 'You give them something to eat.'

They answered, 'We have only five loaves of bread and two fish - unless we go and buy food for all this crowd.' ¹⁴ (About five thousand men were there.)

But he said to his disciples, 'Make them sit down in groups of about fifty each.' ¹⁵ The disciples did so, and everyone sat down.

¹⁶ Taking the five loaves and the two fish and looking up to heaven, he gave thanks and broke them. Then he gave them to the disciples to distribute to the people. ¹⁷ They all ate and were satisfied, and the disciples picked up twelve basketfuls of broken pieces that were left over.

Peter declares that Jesus is the Messiah

¹⁸ Once when Jesus was praying in private and his disciples were with him, he asked them, 'Who do the crowds say I am?'

¹⁹ They replied, 'Some say John the Baptist; others say Elijah; and still others, that one of the prophets of long ago has come back to life.'

²⁰ 'But what about you?' he asked. 'Who do you say I am?'

Peter answered, 'God's Messiah.'

Jesus predicts his death

²¹ Jesus strictly warned them not to tell this to anyone. ²² And he said, 'The Son of Man must suffer many things and be rejected by the elders, the chief priests and the teachers of the law, and he must be killed and on the third day be raised to life.'

²³ Then he said to them all: 'Whoever wants to be my disciple must

deny themselves and take up their cross daily and follow me. ²⁴ For whoever wants to save their life will lose it, but whoever loses their life for me will save it. ²⁵ What good is it for someone to gain the whole world, and yet lose or forfeit their very self? ²⁶ Whoever is ashamed of me and my words, the Son of Man will be ashamed of them when he comes in his glory and in the glory of the Father and of the holy angels.

²⁷ 'Truly I tell you, some who are standing here will not taste death before they see the kingdom of God.'

The transfiguration

²⁸ About eight days after Jesus said this, he took Peter, John and James with him and went up onto a mountain to pray. ²⁹ As he was praying, the appearance of his face changed, and his clothes became as bright as a flash of lightning. ³⁰ Two men, Moses and Elijah, appeared in glorious splendour, talking with Jesus. ³¹ They spoke about his departure, which he was about to bring to fulfilment at Jerusalem. ³² Peter and his companions were very sleepy, but when they became fully awake, they saw his glory and the two men standing with him. ³³ As the men were leaving Jesus, Peter said to him, 'Master, it is good for us to be here. Let us put up three shelters - one for you, one for Moses and one for Elijah.' (He did not know what he was saying.)

³⁴ While he was speaking, a cloud appeared and covered them, and they were afraid as they entered the cloud. ³⁵ A voice came from the cloud, saying, 'This is my Son, whom I have chosen; listen to him.' ³⁶ When the voice had spoken, they found that Jesus was alone. The disciples kept this to themselves and did not tell anyone at that time what they had seen.

Jesus heals a demon-possessed boy

37 The next day, when they came down from the mountain, a large crowd met him. 38 A man in the crowd called out, 'Teacher, I beg you to look at my son, for he is my only child. 39 A spirit seizes him and he suddenly screams; it throws him into convulsions so that he foams at the mouth. It scarcely ever leaves him and is destroying him. 40 I begged your disciples to drive it out, but they could not.'

41 'You unbelieving and perverse generation,' Jesus replied, 'how long shall I stay with you and put up with you? Bring your son here.'

42 Even while the boy was coming, the demon threw him to the ground in a convulsion. But Jesus rebuked the impure spirit, healed the boy and gave him back to his father. 43 And they were all amazed at the greatness of God.

Jesus predicts his death a second time

While everyone was marvelling at all that Jesus did, he said to his disciples, 44 'Listen carefully to what I am about to tell you: The Son of Man is going to be delivered into the hands of men.' 45 But they did not understand what this meant. It was hidden from them, so that they did not grasp it, and they were afraid to ask him about it.

46 An argument started among the disciples as to which of them would be the greatest. 47 Jesus, knowing their thoughts, took a little child and had him stand beside him. 48 Then he said to them, 'Whoever welcomes this little child in my name welcomes me; and whoever welcomes me welcomes the one who sent me. For it is the one who is least among you all who is the greatest.'

49 'Master,' said John, 'we saw someone driving out demons in your name and we tried to stop him, because he is not one of us.'

50 'Do not stop him,' Jesus said, 'for whoever is not against you is for you.'

Samaritan opposition

⁵¹ As the time approached for him to be taken up to heaven, Jesus resolutely set out for Jerusalem. ⁵² And he sent messengers on ahead, who went into a Samaritan village to get things ready for him; ⁵³ but the people there did not welcome him, because he was heading for Jerusalem. ⁵⁴ When the disciples James and John saw this, they asked, 'Lord, do you want us to call fire down from heaven to destroy them?'

⁵⁵ But Jesus turned and rebuked them. ⁵⁶ Then he and his disciples went to another village.

The cost of following Jesus

⁵⁷ As they were walking along the road, a man said to him, 'I will follow you wherever you go.'

⁵⁸ Jesus replied, 'Foxes have dens and birds have nests, but the Son of Man has nowhere to lay his head.'

⁵⁹ He said to another man, 'Follow me.'

But he replied, 'Lord, first let me go and bury my father.'

⁶⁰ Jesus said to him, 'Let the dead bury their own dead, but you go and proclaim the kingdom of God.'

⁶¹ Still another said, 'I will follow you, Lord; but first let me go back and say goodbye to my family.'

⁶² Jesus replied, 'No one who puts a hand to the plough and looks back is fit for service in the kingdom of God.'

Jesus sends out the seventy-two

10 After this the Lord appointed seventy-two others and sent them two by two ahead of him to every town and place where he was about to go. ² He told them, 'The harvest is plentiful, but the workers are few. Ask the Lord of the harvest, therefore, to send out workers into his harvest field. ³ Go! I am sending you out like lambs among wolves. ⁴ Do not take a purse or bag or sandals; and do not greet anyone on the road.

⁵ 'When you enter a house, first say, "Peace to this house." ⁶ If someone who promotes peace is there, your peace will rest on them; if not, it will return to you. ⁷ Stay there, eating and drinking whatever they give you, for the worker deserves his wages. Do not move around from house to house.

⁸ 'When you enter a town and are welcomed, eat what is offered to you. ⁹ Heal those there who are ill and tell them, "The kingdom of God has come near to you." ¹⁰ But when you enter a town and are not welcomed, go into its streets and say, ¹¹ "Even the dust of your town we wipe from our feet as a warning to you. Yet be sure of this: the kingdom of God has come near." ¹² I tell you, it will be more bearable on that day for Sodom than for that town.¹³ 'Woe to you, Chorazin! Woe to you, Bethsaida! For if the miracles that were performed in you had been performed in Tyre and Sidon, they would have repented long ago, sitting in sackcloth and ashes. ¹⁴ But it will be more bearable for Tyre and Sidon at the judgment than for you.

¹⁵ And you, Capernaum, will you be lifted to the heavens? No, you will go down to Hades.

¹⁶ 'Whoever listens to you listens to me; whoever rejects you rejects me; but whoever rejects me rejects him who sent me.'

¹⁷ The seventy-two returned with joy and said, 'Lord, even the demons submit to us in your name.'

¹⁸ He replied, 'I saw Satan fall like lightning from heaven. ¹⁹ I have given you authority to trample on snakes and scorpions and to overcome all the power of the enemy; nothing will harm you.

²⁰ However, do not rejoice that the spirits submit to you, but rejoice that your names are written in heaven.'

²¹ At that time Jesus, full of joy through the Holy Spirit, said, 'I praise you, Father, Lord of heaven and earth, because you have hidden these things from the wise and learned, and revealed them to little children. Yes, Father, for this is what you were pleased to do.

²² 'All things have been committed to me by my Father. No one knows who the Son is except the Father, and no one knows who the Father is except the Son and those to whom the Son chooses to reveal him.'

²³ Then he turned to his disciples and said privately, 'Blessed are the eyes that see what you see. ²⁴ For I tell you that many prophets and kings wanted to see what you see but did not see it, and to hear what you hear but did not hear it.'

The parable of the good Samaritan

²⁵ On one occasion an expert in the law stood up to test Jesus. 'Teacher,' he asked, 'what must I do to inherit eternal life?'

²⁶ 'What is written in the Law?' he replied. 'How do you read it?'

²⁷ He answered, '"Love the Lord your God with all your heart and with all your soul and with all your strength and with all your mind"; and, "Love your neighbour as yourself."'

²⁸ 'You have answered correctly,' Jesus replied. 'Do this and you will live.'

²⁹ But he wanted to justify himself, so he asked Jesus, 'And who is my neighbour?'

³⁰ In reply Jesus said: 'A man was going down from Jerusalem to Jericho, when he was attacked by robbers. They stripped him of his clothes, beat him and went away, leaving him half dead. ³¹ A priest happened to be going down the same road, and when he saw the man, he passed by on the other side. ³² So too, a Levite, when he came to the place and saw him, passed by on the other side. ³³ But a Samaritan, as he travelled, came where the man was; and when he saw him, he took pity on him. ³⁴ He went to him and bandaged his wounds, pouring on oil and wine. Then he put the man on his own donkey, brought him to an inn and took care of him. ³⁵ The next day he took out two denarii and gave them to the innkeeper. "Look after him," he said, "and when I return, I will reimburse you for any extra

expense you may have."³⁶ 'Which of these three do you think was a neighbour to the man who fell into the hands of robbers?'

³⁷ The expert in the law replied, 'The one who had mercy on him.'

Jesus told him, 'Go and do likewise.'

At the home of Martha and Mary

³⁸ As Jesus and his disciples were on their way, he came to a village where a woman named Martha opened her home to him. ³⁹ She had a sister called Mary, who sat at the Lord's feet listening to what he said. ⁴⁰ But Martha was distracted by all the preparations that had to be made. She came to him and asked, 'Lord, don't you care that my sister has left me to do the work by myself? Tell her to help me!'

⁴¹ 'Martha, Martha,' the Lord answered, 'you are worried and upset about many things, ⁴² but few things are needed - or indeed only one. Mary has chosen what is better, and it will not be taken away from her.'

Jesus' teaching on prayer

11 One day Jesus was praying in a certain place. When he finished, one of his disciples said to him, 'Lord, teach us to pray, just as John taught his disciples.'

² He said to them, 'When you pray, say:

"'Father,
hallowed be your name,
your kingdom come.
³ Give us each day our daily bread.
⁴ Forgive us our sins,
    for we also forgive everyone who sins against us.
And lead us not into temptation.'"

⁵ Then Jesus said to them, 'Suppose you have a friend, and you

go to him at midnight and say, "Friend, lend me three loaves of bread;

[6] a friend of mine on a journey has come to me, and I have no food to offer him." [7] And suppose the one inside answers, "Don't bother me. The door is already locked, and my children and I are in bed. I can't get up and give you anything." [8] I tell you, even though he will not get up and give you the bread because of friendship, yet because of your shameless audacity he will surely get up and give you as much as you need.

[9] 'So I say to you: ask and it will be given to you; seek and you will find; knock and the door will be opened to you. [10] For everyone who asks receives; the one who seeks finds; and to the one who knocks, the door will be opened.

[11] 'Which of you fathers, if your son asks for a fish, will give him a snake instead? [12] Or if he asks for an egg, will give him a scorpion?

[13] If you then, though you are evil, know how to give good gifts to your children, how much more will your Father in heaven give the Holy Spirit to those who ask him!'

Jesus and Beelzebul

[14] Jesus was driving out a demon that was mute. When the demon left, the man who had been mute spoke, and the crowd was amazed. [15] But some of them said, 'By Beelzebul, the prince of demons, he is driving out demons.' [16] Others tested him by asking for a sign from heaven.

[17] Jesus knew their thoughts and said to them: 'Any kingdom divided against itself will be ruined, and a house divided against itself will fall. [18] If Satan is divided against himself, how can his kingdom stand? I say this because you claim that I drive out demons by Beelzebul. [19] Now if I drive out demons by Beelzebul, by whom do your followers drive them out? So then, they will be your judges.

[20] But if I drive out demons by the finger of God, then the kingdom of God has come upon you.

²¹ 'When a strong man, fully armed, guards his own house, his possessions are safe. ²² But when someone stronger attacks and overpowers him, he takes away the armour in which the man trusted and divides up his plunder.

²³ 'Whoever is not with me is against me, and whoever does not gather with me scatters.

²⁴ 'When an impure spirit comes out of a person, it goes through arid places seeking rest and does not find it. Then it says, "I will return to the house I left." ²⁵ When it arrives, it finds the house swept clean and put in order. ²⁶ Then it goes and takes seven other spirits more wicked than itself, and they go in and live there. And the final condition of that person is worse than the first.'

²⁷ As Jesus was saying these things, a woman in the crowd called out, 'Blessed is the mother who gave you birth and nursed you.'

²⁸ He replied, 'Blessed rather are those who hear the word of God and obey it.'

The sign of Jonah

²⁹ As the crowds increased, Jesus said, 'This is a wicked generation. It asks for a sign, but none will be given it except the sign of Jonah. ³⁰ For as Jonah was a sign to the Ninevites, so also will the Son of Man be to this generation. ³¹ The Queen of the South will rise at the judgment with the people of this generation and condemn them, for she came from the ends of the earth to listen to Solomon's wisdom; and now something greater than Solomon is here. ³² The men of Nineveh will stand up at the judgment with this generation and condemn it, for they repented at the preaching of Jonah; and now something greater than Jonah is here.

The lamp of the body

³³ 'No one lights a lamp and puts it in a place where it will be hidden, or under a bowl. Instead they put it on its stand, so that those who

come in may see the light. ³⁴ Your eye is the lamp of your body. When your eyes are healthy, your whole body also is full of light. But when they are unhealthy, your body also is full of darkness. ³⁵ See to it, then, that the light within you is not darkness. ³⁶ Therefore, if your whole body is full of light, and no part of it dark, it will be just as full of light as when a lamp shines its light on you.'

Woes on the Pharisees and the experts in the law

³⁷ When Jesus had finished speaking, a Pharisee invited him to eat with him; so he went in and reclined at the table. ³⁸ But the Pharisee was surprised when he noticed that Jesus did not first wash before the meal.

³⁹ Then the Lord said to him, 'Now then, you Pharisees clean the outside of the cup and dish, but inside you are full of greed and wickedness. ⁴⁰ You foolish people! Did not the one who made the outside make the inside also? ⁴¹ But now as for what is inside you - be generous to the poor, and everything will be clean for you.

⁴² 'Woe to you Pharisees, because you give God a tenth of your mint, rue and all other kinds of garden herbs, but you neglect justice and the love of God. You should have practiced the latter without leaving the former undone.

⁴³ 'Woe to you Pharisees, because you love the most important seats in the synagogues and respectful greetings in the marketplaces.

⁴⁴ 'Woe to you, because you are like unmarked graves, which people walk over without knowing it.'

⁴⁵ One of the experts in the law answered him, 'Teacher, when you say these things, you insult us also.'

⁴⁶ Jesus replied, 'And you experts in the law, woe to you, because you load people down with burdens they can hardly carry, and you yourselves will not lift one finger to help them.

⁴⁷ 'Woe to you, because you build tombs for the prophets, and

it was your ancestors who killed them. ⁴⁸ So you testify that you approve of what your ancestors did; they killed the prophets, and you build their tombs. ⁴⁹ Because of this, God in his wisdom said, "I will send them prophets and apostles, some of whom they will kill and others they will persecute." ⁵⁰ Therefore this generation will be held responsible for the blood of all the prophets that has been shed since the beginning of the world, ⁵¹ from the blood of Abel to the blood of Zechariah, who was killed between the altar and the sanctuary. Yes, I tell you, this generation will be held responsible for it all.

⁵² 'Woe to you experts in the law, because you have taken away the key to knowledge. You yourselves have not entered, and you have hindered those who were entering.'

⁵³ When Jesus went outside, the Pharisees and the teachers of the law began to oppose him fiercely and to besiege him with questions, ⁵⁴ waiting to catch him in something he might say.

Warnings and encouragements

12 Meanwhile, when a crowd of many thousands had gathered, so that they were trampling on one another, Jesus began to speak first to his disciples, saying: 'Be on your guard against the yeast of the Pharisees, which is hypocrisy. ² There is nothing concealed that will not be disclosed, or hidden that will not be made known. ³ What you have said in the dark will be heard in the daylight, and what you have whispered in the ear in the inner rooms will be proclaimed from the roofs.

⁴ 'I tell you, my friends, do not be afraid of those who kill the body and after that can do no more. ⁵ But I will show you whom you should fear: fear him who, after your body has been killed, has authority to throw you into hell. Yes, I tell you, fear him. ⁶ Are not five sparrows sold for two pennies? Yet not one of them is forgotten by God. ⁷ Indeed, the very hairs of your head are all numbered. Don't be afraid; you are

worth more than many sparrows.

⁸ 'I tell you, whoever publicly acknowledges me before others, the Son of Man will also acknowledge before the angels of God. ⁹ But whoever disowns me before others will be disowned before the angels of God. ¹⁰ And everyone who speaks a word against the Son of Man will be forgiven, but anyone who blasphemes against the Holy Spirit will not be forgiven.

¹¹ 'When you are brought before synagogues, rulers and authorities, do not worry about how you will defend yourselves or what you will say, ¹² for the Holy Spirit will teach you at that time what you should say.'

The parable of the rich fool

¹³ Someone in the crowd said to him, 'Teacher, tell my brother to divide the inheritance with me.'

¹⁴ Jesus replied, 'Man, who appointed me a judge or an arbiter between you?' ¹⁵ Then he said to them, 'Watch out! Be on your guard against all kinds of greed; life does not consist in an abundance of possessions.'

¹⁶ And he told them this parable: 'The ground of a certain rich man yielded an abundant harvest. ¹⁷ He thought to himself, "What shall I do? I have no place to store my crops."

¹⁸ 'Then he said, "This is what I'll do. I will tear down my barns and build bigger ones, and there I will store my surplus grain. ¹⁹ And I'll say to myself, 'You have plenty of grain laid up for many years. Take life easy; eat, drink and be merry.'"

²⁰ 'But God said to him, "You fool! This very night your life will be demanded from you. Then who will get what you have prepared for yourself?"

²¹ 'This is how it will be with whoever stores up things for themselves but is not rich toward God.'

Do not worry

²² Then Jesus said to his disciples: 'Therefore I tell you, do not worry about your life, what you will eat; or about your body, what you will wear. ²³ For life is more than food, and the body more than clothes. ²⁴ Consider the ravens: They do not sow or reap, they have no storeroom or barn; yet God feeds them. And how much more valuable you are than birds! ²⁵ Who of you by worrying can add a single hour to your life? ²⁶ Since you cannot do this very little thing, why do you worry about the rest?

²⁷ 'Consider how the wild flowers grow. They do not labour or spin. Yet I tell you, not even Solomon in all his splendour was dressed like one of these. ²⁸ If that is how God clothes the grass of the field, which is here today, and tomorrow is thrown into the fire, how much more will he clothe you - you of little faith! ²⁹ And do not set your heart on what you will eat or drink; do not worry about it. ³⁰ For the pagan world runs after all such things, and your Father knows that you need them. ³¹ But seek his kingdom, and these things will be given to you as well.

³² 'Do not be afraid, little flock, for your Father has been pleased to give you the kingdom. ³³ Sell your possessions and give to the poor. Provide purses for yourselves that will not wear out, a treasure in heaven that will never fail, where no thief comes near and no moth destroys. ³⁴ For where your treasure is, there your heart will be also.

Watchfulness

³⁵ 'Be dressed ready for service and keep your lamps burning, ³⁶ like servants waiting for their master to return from a wedding banquet, so that when he comes and knocks they can immediately open the door for him. ³⁷ It will be good for those servants whose master finds them watching when he comes. Truly I tell you, he will dress himself to serve, will have them recline at the table and will come and wait on them. ³⁸ It will be good for those servants whose

master finds them ready, even if he comes in the middle of the night or toward daybreak. ³⁹ But understand this: If the owner of the house had known at what hour the thief was coming, he would not have let his house be broken into. ⁴⁰ You also must be ready, because the Son of Man will come at an hour when you do not expect him.'

⁴¹ Peter asked, 'Lord, are you telling this parable to us, or to everyone?'

⁴² The Lord answered, 'Who then is the faithful and wise manager, whom the master puts in charge of his servants to give them their food allowance at the proper time? ⁴³ It will be good for that servant whom the master finds doing so when he returns. ⁴⁴ Truly I tell you, he will put him in charge of all his possessions. ⁴⁵ But suppose the servant says to himself, "My master is taking a long time in coming," and he then begins to beat the other servants, both men and women, and to eat and drink and get drunk. ⁴⁶ The master of that servant will come on a day when he does not expect him and at an hour he is not aware of. He will cut him to pieces and assign him a place with the unbelievers.

⁴⁷ 'The servant who knows the master's will and does not get ready or does not do what the master wants will be beaten with many blows. ⁴⁸ But the one who does not know and does things deserving punishment will be beaten with few blows. From everyone who has been given much, much will be demanded; and from the one who has been entrusted with much, much more will be asked.

Not peace but division

⁴⁹ 'I have come to bring fire on the earth, and how I wish it were already kindled! ⁵⁰ But I have a baptism to undergo, and what constraint I am under until it is completed! ⁵¹ Do you think I came to bring peace on earth? No, I tell you, but division. ⁵² From now on there will be five in one family divided against each other, three against two and two against three. ⁵³ They will be divided, father against son and son against father, mother against daughter and daughter against

mother, mother-in-law against daughter-in-law and daughter-in-law against mother-in-law.'

Interpreting the times

54 He said to the crowd: 'When you see a cloud rising in the west, immediately you say, "It's going to rain," and it does. 55 And when the south wind blows, you say, "It's going to be hot," and it is. 56 Hypocrites! You know how to interpret the appearance of the earth and the sky. How is it that you don't know how to interpret this present time?

57 'Why don't you judge for yourselves what is right? 58 As you are going with your adversary to the magistrate, try hard to be reconciled on the way, or your adversary may drag you off to the judge, and the judge turn you over to the officer, and the officer throw you into prison. 59 I tell you, you will not get out until you have paid the last penny.'

Repent or perish

13 Now there were some present at that time who told Jesus about the Galileans whose blood Pilate had mixed with their sacrifices. 2 Jesus answered, 'Do you think that these Galileans were worse sinners than all the other Galileans because they suffered this way? 3 I tell you, no! But unless you repent, you too will all perish. 4 Or those eighteen who died when the tower in Siloam fell on them - do you think they were more guilty than all the others living in Jerusalem? 5 I tell you, no! But unless you repent, you too will all perish.'

6 Then he told this parable: 'A man had a fig tree growing in his vineyard, and he went to look for fruit on it but did not find any. 7 So he said to the man who took care of the vineyard, "For three years now I've been coming to look for fruit on this fig tree and haven't found any. Cut it down! Why should it use up the soil?"

8 "'Sir,' the man replied, "leave it alone for one more year, and I'll dig around it and fertilise it. 9 If it bears fruit next year, fine! If not, then cut it down."'

Jesus heals a crippled woman on the Sabbath

¹⁰ On a Sabbath Jesus was teaching in one of the synagogues, ¹¹ and a woman was there who had been crippled by a spirit for eighteen years. She was bent over and could not straighten up at all. ¹² When Jesus saw her, he called her forward and said to her, 'Woman, you are set free from your infirmity.' ¹³ Then he put his hands on her, and immediately she straightened up and praised God.

¹⁴ Indignant because Jesus had healed on the Sabbath, the synagogue leader said to the people, 'There are six days for work. So come and be healed on those days, not on the Sabbath.'

¹⁵ The Lord answered him, 'You hypocrites! Doesn't each of you on the Sabbath untie your ox or donkey from the stall and lead it out to give it water? ¹⁶ Then should not this woman, a daughter of Abraham, whom Satan has kept bound for eighteen long years, be set free on the Sabbath day from what bound her?'

¹⁷ When he said this, all his opponents were humiliated, but the people were delighted with all the wonderful things he was doing.

The parables of the mustard seed and the yeast

¹⁸ Then Jesus asked, 'What is the kingdom of God like? What shall I compare it to? ¹⁹ It is like a mustard seed, which a man took and planted in his garden. It grew and became a tree, and the birds perched in its branches.'

²⁰ Again he asked, 'What shall I compare the kingdom of God to?

²¹ It is like yeast that a woman took and mixed into about sixty pounds of flour until it worked all through the dough.'

The narrow door

²² Then Jesus went through the towns and villages, teaching as he made his way to Jerusalem. ²³ Someone asked him, 'Lord, are only a few people going to be saved?'

He said to them, ²⁴ 'Make every effort to enter through the narrow door, because many, I tell you, will try to enter and will not be able to. ²⁵ Once the owner of the house gets up and closes the door, you will stand outside knocking and pleading, "Sir, open the door for us."

'But he will answer, "I don't know you or where you come from."

²⁶ 'Then you will say, "We ate and drank with you, and you taught in our streets."

²⁷ 'But he will reply, "I don't know you or where you come from. Away from me, all you evildoers!"

²⁸ 'There will be weeping there, and gnashing of teeth, when you see Abraham, Isaac and Jacob and all the prophets in the kingdom of God, but you yourselves thrown out. ²⁹ People will come from east and west and north and south, and will take their places at the feast in the kingdom of God. ³⁰ Indeed there are those who are last who will be first, and first who will be last.'

Jesus' sorrow for Jerusalem

³¹ At that time some Pharisees came to Jesus and said to him, 'Leave this place and go somewhere else. Herod wants to kill you.'

³² He replied, 'Go and tell that fox, "I will keep on driving out demons and healing people today and tomorrow, and on the third day I will reach my goal." ³³ In any case, I must press on today and tomorrow and the next day - for surely no prophet can die outside Jerusalem!

³⁴ 'Jerusalem, Jerusalem, you who kill the prophets and stone those sent to you, how often I have longed to gather your children together, as a hen gathers her chicks under her wings, and you were not willing. ³⁵ Look, your house is left to you desolate. I tell you, you will not see me again until you say, "Blessed is he who comes in the name of the Lord."'

Jesus at a Pharisee's house

14 One Sabbath, when Jesus went to eat in the house of a prominent Pharisee, he was being carefully watched.

² There in front of him was a man suffering from abnormal swelling of his body. ³ Jesus asked the Pharisees and experts in the law, 'Is it lawful to heal on the Sabbath or not?' ⁴ But they remained silent. So taking hold of the man, he healed him and sent him on his way.

⁵ Then he asked them, 'If one of you has a child or an ox that falls into a well on the Sabbath day, will you not immediately pull it out?'

⁶ And they had nothing to say.

⁷ When he noticed how the guests picked the places of honour at the table, he told them this parable: ⁸ 'When someone invites you to a wedding feast, do not take the place of honour, for a person more distinguished than you may have been invited. ⁹ If so, the host who invited both of you will come and say to you, "Give this person your seat." Then, humiliated, you will have to take the least important place. ¹⁰ But when you are invited, take the lowest place, so that when your host comes, he will say to you, "Friend, move up to a better place." Then you will be honoured in the presence of all the other guests.

¹¹ For all those who exalt themselves will be humbled, and those who humble themselves will be exalted.'

¹² Then Jesus said to his host, 'When you give a luncheon or dinner, do not invite your friends, your brothers or sisters, your relatives, or your rich neighbours; if you do, they may invite you back and so you will be repaid. ¹³ But when you give a banquet, invite the poor, the crippled, the lame, the blind, ¹⁴ and you will be blessed. Although they cannot repay you, you will be repaid at the resurrection of the righteous.'

The parable of the great banquet

¹⁵ When one of those at the table with him heard this, he said to Jesus, 'Blessed is the one who will eat at the feast in the kingdom of God.'

¹⁶ Jesus replied: 'A certain man was preparing a great banquet and invited many guests. ¹⁷ At the time of the banquet he sent his servant to tell those who had been invited, "Come, for everything is now ready."

¹⁸ 'But they all alike began to make excuses. The first said, "I have just bought a field, and I must go and see it. Please excuse me."

¹⁹ 'Another said, "I have just bought five yoke of oxen, and I'm on my way to try them out. Please excuse me."

²⁰ 'Still another said, "I just got married, so I can't come."

²¹ 'The servant came back and reported this to his master. Then the owner of the house became angry and ordered his servant, "Go out quickly into the streets and alleys of the town and bring in the poor, the crippled, the blind and the lame."

²² "Sir," the servant said, "what you ordered has been done, but there is still room."

²³ 'Then the master told his servant, "Go out to the roads and country lanes and compel them to come in, so that my house will be full. ²⁴ I tell you, not one of those who were invited will get a taste of my banquet."'

The cost of being a disciple

[25] Large crowds were traveling with Jesus, and turning to them he said: [26] 'If anyone comes to me and does not hate father and mother, wife and children, brothers and sisters - yes, even their own life - such a person cannot be my disciple. [27] And whoever does not carry their cross and follow me cannot be my disciple.

[28] 'Suppose one of you wants to build a tower. Won't you first sit down and estimate the cost to see if you have enough money to complete it? [29] For if you lay the foundation and are not able to finish it, everyone who sees it will ridicule you, [30] saying, "This person began to build and wasn't able to finish."

³¹ 'Or suppose a king is about to go to war against another king. Won't he first sit down and consider whether he is able with ten thousand men to oppose the one coming against him with twenty thousand? ³² If he is not able, he will send a delegation while the other is still a long way off and will ask for terms of peace. ³³ In the same way, those of you who do not give up everything you have cannot be my disciples.

³⁴ 'Salt is good, but if it loses its saltiness, how can it be made salty again? ³⁵ It is fit neither for the soil nor for the manure pile; it is thrown out.

'Whoever has ears to hear, let them hear.'

Freedom

Study 3

LUKE 15:1-2 & 11-32

Each of us has a vision of how we would like our life to be. But sometimes that life can feel out of reach.

1. What stops people from living the life they want?

Since meeting the widow, Jesus has continued to transform the lives of those on the margins of society. As he has met their needs, he has gained attention. He has also gained criticism from the religious leaders.

We rejoin Jesus as he addresses a crowd.

READ LUKE 15:1-2

> *'Tax collectors and sinners' are outcasts, shunned as those who fail to meet society's ethical and religious expectations. By contrast, the 'Pharisees and teachers of the law' are the religious elite, who tirelessly give themselves to God's law and to ethical living.*

2. **What does Luke tell us about these two groups? What does this suggest about their motivation to come and listen to Jesus?**

> *Keep these groups in mind as we read on.*

READ LUKE 15:11-12

> *The son would ordinarily have received his inheritance after the father's death. To meet the son's demand, it would have cost the father financially. It would also have cost him socially. As neighbours looked on, the father would have been left humiliated.*

3. **What do you think the younger son's request reveals about how he views his father?**

4. **How do you imagine the father is left feeling after his son's request?**

The parable of the lost sheep

15 Now the tax collectors and sinners were all gathering around to hear Jesus. ² But the Pharisees and the teachers of the law muttered, 'This man welcomes sinners and eats with them.

³ Then Jesus told them this parable: ⁴ 'Suppose one of you has a hundred sheep and loses one of them. Doesn't he leave the ninety-nine in the open country and go after the lost sheep until he finds it? ⁵ And when he finds it, he joyfully puts it on his shoulders ⁶ and goes home. Then he calls his friends and neighbours together and says, "Rejoice with me; I have found my lost sheep."

⁷ I tell you that in the same way there will be more rejoicing in heaven over one sinner who repents than over ninety-nine righteous persons who do not need to repent.

The parable of the lost coin

⁸ 'Or suppose a woman has ten silver coins and loses one. Doesn't she light a lamp, sweep the house and search carefully until she finds it? ⁹ And when she finds it, she calls her friends and neighbours together and says, "Rejoice with me; I have found my lost coin." ¹⁰ In the same way, I tell you, there is rejoicing in the presence of the angels of God over one sinner who repents.'

The parable of the lost son

¹¹ Jesus continued: 'There was a man who had two sons. ¹² The younger one said to his father, "Father, give me my share of the estate." So he divided his property between them.

Pharisee - community leaders who enforced strict adherence to religious laws.
Teacher of the Law - theologians who interpreted the Jewish scriptures.
Share of the estate - a portion of an inheritance.

READ LUKE 15:13-19

The younger son seeks freedom away from his father, but ends up trapped, ashamed, and hungry. Sitting amongst the pigs, he has hit an all-time low. And it's there that the son re-evaluates his decisions and decides to return home.

5. **What mistakes do you think the son can now see he has made?**

6. **As the younger son plans to return home, how does he hope to repair his relationship with his father?**

READ LUKE 15:20-24

7. **Imagine the son as he spots his father's house in the distance. What do you think the son's appearance is like? What do you think he is feeling?**

8. **How do the son's expectations of his father contrast with what actually happens? What does this tell us about how the father views his son?**

The father is so overjoyed that he throws a lavish party. All his actions communicate to his son, and to those watching, that he is forgiven and welcome at the family table.

¹³ 'Not long after that, the younger son got together all he had, set off for a distant country and there squandered his wealth in wild living. ¹⁴ After he had spent everything, there was a severe famine in that whole country, and he began to be in need. ¹⁵ So he went and hired himself out to a citizen of that country, who sent him to his fields to feed pigs. ¹⁶ He longed to fill his stomach with the pods that the pigs were eating, but no one gave him anything.

¹⁷ 'When he came to his senses, he said, "How many of my father's hired servants have food to spare, and here I am starving to death! ¹⁸ I will set out and go back to my father and say to him: Father, I have sinned against heaven and against you. ¹⁹ I am no longer worthy to be called your son; make me like one of your hired servants."

²⁰ So he got up and went to his father.

'But while he was still a long way off, his father saw him and was filled with compassion for him; he ran to his son, threw his arms around him and kissed him.

²¹ 'The son said to him, "Father, I have sinned against heaven and against you. I am no longer worthy to be called your son."

²² 'But the father said to his servants, "Quick! Bring the best robe and put it on him. Put a ring on his finger and sandals on his feet. ²³ Bring the fattened calf and kill it. Let's have a feast and celebrate. ²⁴ For this son of mine was dead and is alive again; he was lost and is found." So they began to celebrate.

Jesus now draws our attention to the older son.

9.   **Why do you think the older brother responds as he does? Do you think his response is reasonable?**

10.   **Read verse 29. What does this reveal about how the older son views his relationship with his father? What does he fail to see?**

> *The younger son shamed the father by running away. Now the older son shames him by refusing to come in and join the party. Given how they have treated their father, neither son is worthy of a seat at the banquet.*
>
> *At the beginning of the story, the rebellious younger son is more obviously lost. Yet as the story closes, it is the older son who is in greater danger of being alienated from his father. He is lost.*
>
> *But in his compassion, the father goes out to both sons. He wants them at his banquet.*

11.   **Jesus is saying that this father represents God. How does the father compare with what you imagine God to be like?**

²⁵ 'Meanwhile, the elder son was in the field. When he came near the house, he heard music and dancing. ²⁶ So he called one of the servants and asked him what was going on. ²⁷ "Your brother has come," he replied, "and your father has killed the fattened calf because he has him back safe and sound."

²⁸ 'The elder brother became angry and refused to go in. So his father went out and pleaded with him. ²⁹ But he answered his father, "Look! All these years I've been slaving for you and never disobeyed your orders. Yet you never gave me even a young goat so I could celebrate with my friends. ³⁰ But when this son of yours who has squandered your property with prostitutes comes home, you kill the fattened calf for him!" ³¹ "'My son," the father said, "you are always with me, and everything I have is yours. ³² But we had to celebrate and be glad, because this brother of yours was dead and is alive again; he was lost and is found."'

Process **together**

Jesus speaks to a crowd of younger sons (rebellious tax collectors) and older sons (hard-working Pharisees).

Both groups are lost. They both believe they will find real life away from God.

We are invited to see ourselves in these two groups. Like the tax collectors we look for freedom away from God. Or like the Pharisees, rather than simply accepting God's love, we think we can earn it by our own work. Whatever form it takes, our resistance dishonours the God we were made to know.

12.   Which of the two groups in the crowd do you relate to more?

Jesus is making a bold statement. He says that apart from God, we can never know true life.

Instead, we find true life and freedom when we 'come to our senses' and return home to God. And just like the Father, God will welcome us back with compassion and celebration, however lost we might be.

13.   How does it make you feel knowing that God wants to welcome you in this way?

The parable of the shrewd manager

16 Jesus told his disciples: 'There was a rich man whose manager was accused of wasting his possessions. ² So he called him in and asked him, "What is this I hear about you? Give an account of your management, because you cannot be manager any longer."

³ 'The manager said to himself, "What shall I do now? My master is taking away my job. I'm not strong enough to dig, and I'm ashamed to beg – ⁴ I know what I'll do so that, when I lose my job here, people will welcome me into their houses."

⁵ 'So he called in each one of his master's debtors. He asked the first, "How much do you owe my master?"

⁶ '"Three thousand litres of olive oil," he replied.

'The manager told him, "Take your bill, sit down quickly, and make it fifteen hundred."

⁷ 'Then he asked the second, "And how much do you owe?"

'"Thirty tons of wheat," he replied.

'He told him, "Take your bill and make it twenty-four."

⁸ 'The master commended the dishonest manager because he had acted shrewdly. For the people of this world are more shrewd in dealing with their own kind than are the people of the light. ⁹ I tell you, use worldly wealth to gain friends for yourselves, so that when it is gone, you will be welcomed into eternal dwellings.

¹⁰ 'Whoever can be trusted with very little can also be trusted with much, and whoever is dishonest with very little will also be dishonest with much. ¹¹ So if you have not been trustworthy in handling worldly wealth, who will trust you with true riches? ¹² And if you have not been trustworthy with someone else's property, who will give you property of your own? ¹³ 'No one can serve two masters. Either you will hate the one and love the other, or you will be devoted to the one and despise the other. You cannot serve both God and money.'

¹⁴ The Pharisees, who loved money, heard all this and were

snecring at Jesus. [15] He said to them, 'You are the ones who justify yourselves in the eyes of others, but God knows your hearts. What people value highly is detestable in God's sight.

Additional teachings

[16] 'The Law and the Prophets were proclaimed until John. Since that time, the good news of the kingdom of God is being preached, and everyone is forcing their way into it. [17] It is easier for heaven and earth to disappear than for the least stroke of a pen to drop out of the Law. [18] 'Anyone who divorces his wife and marries another woman commits adultery, and the man who marries a divorced woman commits adultery.

The rich man and Lazarus

[19] 'There was a rich man who was dressed in purple and fine linen and lived in luxury every day. [20] At his gate was laid a beggar named Lazarus, covered with sores [21] and longing to eat what fell from the rich man's table. Even the dogs came and licked his sores.

[22] 'The time came when the beggar died and the angels carried him to Abraham's side. The rich man also died and was buried. [23] In Hades, where he was in torment, he looked up and saw Abraham far away, with Lazarus by his side. [24] So he called to him, "Father Abraham, have pity on me and send Lazarus to dip the tip of his finger in water and cool my tongue, because I am in agony in this fire." [25] 'But Abraham replied, "Son, remember that in your lifetime you received your good things, while Lazarus received bad things, but now he is comforted here and you are in agony. [26] And besides all this, between us and you a great chasm has been set in place, so that those who want to go from here to you cannot, nor can anyone cross over from there to us."

[27] 'He answered, "Then I beg you, father, send Lazarus to my family, [28] for I have five brothers. Let him warn them, so that they will not also

come to this place of torment."

²⁹ 'Abraham replied, "They have Moses and the Prophets; let them listen to them."

³⁰ "No, father Abraham," he said, "but if someone from the dead goes to them, they will repent."

³¹ 'He said to him, "If they do not listen to Moses and the Prophets, they will not be convinced even if someone rises from the dead."'

Sin, faith, duty

17 Jesus said to his disciples: 'Things that cause people to stumble are bound to come, but woe to anyone through whom they come. ² It would be better for them to be thrown into the sea with a millstone tied around their neck than to cause one of these little ones to stumble. ³ So watch yourselves.

'If your brother or sister sins against you, rebuke them; and if they repent, forgive them. ⁴ Even if they sin against you seven times in a day and seven times come back to you saying 'I repent,' you must forgive them.'

⁵ The apostles said to the Lord, 'Increase our faith!'

⁶ He replied, 'If you have faith as small as a mustard seed, you can say to this mulberry tree, 'Be uprooted and planted in the sea,' and it will obey you.

⁷ 'Suppose one of you has a servant ploughing or looking after the sheep. Will he say to the servant when he comes in from the field, "Come along now and sit down to eat"? ⁸ Won't he rather say, "Prepare my supper, get yourself ready and wait on me while I eat and drink; after that you may eat and drink"? ⁹ Will he thank the servant because he did what he was told to do? ¹⁰ So you also, when you have done everything you were told to do, should say, "We are unworthy servants; we have only done our duty."'

Jesus heals ten men with leprosy

[11] Now on his way to Jerusalem, Jesus travelled along the border between Samaria and Galilee. [12] As he was going into a village, ten men who had leprosy met him. They stood at a distance [13] and called out in a loud voice, 'Jesus, Master, have pity on us!'

[14] When he saw them, he said, 'Go, show yourselves to the priests.' And as they went, they were cleansed.

[15] One of them, when he saw he was healed, came back, praising God in a loud voice. [16] He threw himself at Jesus' feet and thanked him - and he was a Samaritan.

[17] Jesus asked, 'Were not all ten cleansed? Where are the other nine? [18] Has no one returned to give praise to God except this foreigner?' [19] Then he said to him, 'Rise and go; your faith has made you well.'

The coming of the kingdom of God

[20] Once, on being asked by the Pharisees when the kingdom of God would come, Jesus replied, 'The coming of the kingdom of God is not something that can be observed, [21] nor will people say, "Here it is," or "There it is," because the kingdom of God is in your midst.'

[22] Then he said to his disciples, 'The time is coming when you will long to see one of the days of the Son of Man, but you will not see it. [23] People will tell you, "There he is!" or "Here he is!" Do not go running off after them. [24] For the Son of Man in his day will be like the lightning, which flashes and lights up the sky from one end to the other. [25] But first he must suffer many things and be rejected by this generation.

[26] 'Just as it was in the days of Noah, so also will it be in the days of the Son of Man. [27] People were eating, drinking, marrying and being given in marriage up to the day Noah entered the ark. Then the flood came and destroyed them all.

[28] 'It was the same in the days of Lot. People were eating and

drinking, buying and selling, planting and building. ²⁹ But the day Lot left Sodom, fire and sulphur rained down from heaven and destroyed them all.

³⁰ 'It will be just like this on the day the Son of Man is revealed.

³¹ On that day no one who is on the housetop, with possessions inside, should go down to get them. Likewise, no one in the field should go back for anything. ³² Remember Lot's wife! ³³ Whoever tries to keep their life will lose it, and whoever loses their life will preserve it. ³⁴ I tell you, on that night two people will be in one bed; one will be taken and the other left. ³⁵ Two women will be grinding grain together; one will be taken and the other left.'

³⁷ 'Where, Lord?' they asked.

He replied, 'Where there is a dead body, there the vultures will gather.'

The parable of the persistent widow

18 Then Jesus told his disciples a parable to show them that they should always pray and not give up. ² He said: 'In a certain town there was a judge who neither feared God nor cared what people thought. ³ And there was a widow in that town who kept coming to him with the plea, 'Grant me justice against my adversary.'

⁴ 'For some time he refused. But finally he said to himself, 'Even though I don't fear God or care what people think, ⁵ yet because this

widow keeps bothering me, I will see that she gets justice, so that she won't eventually come and attack me!"

[6] And the Lord said, 'Listen to what the unjust judge says. [7] And will not God bring about justice for his chosen ones, who cry out to him day and night? Will he keep putting them off? [8] I tell you, he will see that they get justice, and quickly. However, when the Son of Man comes, will he find faith on the earth?'

The parable of the Pharisee and the tax collector

[9] To some who were confident of their own righteousness and looked down on everyone else, Jesus told this parable: [10] 'Two men went up to the temple to pray, one a Pharisee and the other a tax collector. [11] The Pharisee stood by himself and prayed: "God, I thank you that I am not like other people – robbers, evildoers, adulterers – or even like this tax collector. [12] I fast twice a week and give a tenth of all I get."

[13] 'But the tax collector stood at a distance. He would not even look up to heaven, but beat his breast and said, "God, have mercy on me, a sinner."

[14] 'I tell you that this man, rather than the other, went home justified before God. For all those who exalt themselves will be humbled, and those who humble themselves will be exalted.'

PAUSE
Sit in stillness for a moment.

LOOK
Notice what stands out in the artwork.

READ
Read the passage slowly, once or twice.

REFLECT
Use the questions to guide your thoughts and response.

The little children and Jesus

 15 People were also bringing babies to Jesus for him to place his hands on them. When the disciples saw this, they rebuked them.

 16 But Jesus called the children to him and said, 'Let the little children come to me, and do not hinder them, for the kingdom of God belongs to such as these. 17 Truly I tell you, anyone who will not receive the kingdom of God like a little child will never enter it.'

In first-century Palestine, children were given little value.

Yet as Jesus calls these small children to come to him, he wants his disciples to learn something: if you want to belong with Jesus, you need to come to him like these children.

1.   **What do Jesus' words and actions suggest about how Jesus wants us to relate to him?**

2.   **Why do you think Jesus' acceptance of children challenges the disciples?**

3.   **Where do Jesus' words challenge you? In what ways do they sound like good news?**

Look again at the artwork.
Does anything different stand out to you?

The rich and the kingdom of God

[18] A certain ruler asked him, 'Good teacher, what must I do to inherit eternal life?'

[19] 'Why do you call me good?' Jesus answered. 'No one is good - except God alone. [20] You know the commandments: 'You shall not commit adultery, you shall not murder, you shall not steal, you shall not give false testimony, honour your father and mother.''

[21] 'All these I have kept since I was a boy,' he said.

[22] When Jesus heard this, he said to him, 'You still lack one thing. Sell everything you have and give to the poor, and you will have treasure in heaven. Then come, follow me.'

[23] When he heard this, he became very sad, because he was very wealthy. [24] Jesus looked at him and said, 'How hard it is for the rich to enter the kingdom of God! [25] Indeed, it is easier for a camel to go through the eye of a needle than for someone who is rich to enter the kingdom of God.'

[26] Those who heard this asked, 'Who then can be saved?'

27 Jesus replied, 'What is impossible with man is possible with God.'

28 Peter said to him, 'We have left all we had to follow you!'

29 'Truly I tell you,' Jesus said to them, 'no one who has left home or wife or brothers or sisters or parents or children for the sake of the kingdom of God 30 will fail to receive many times as much in this age, and in the age to come eternal life.'

Jesus predicts his death a third time

31 Jesus took the Twelve aside and told them, 'We are going up to Jerusalem, and everything that is written by the prophets about the Son of Man will be fulfilled. 32 He will be delivered over to the Gentiles. They will mock him, insult him and spit on him; 33 they will flog him and kill him. On the third day he will rise again.' 34 The disciples did not understand any of this. Its meaning was hidden from them, and they did not know what he was talking about.

Transformation

Study 4

LUKE 18:35-19:10

When we face problems, some wisdom encourages us to look for hope and strength inside ourselves. We are told that what is inside us is greater than any obstacle we might face.

DISCUSS

1. Do you think there are any obstacles that cannot be overcome by looking within ourselves?

Since his parable of the lost son, Jesus has continued to teach people what it looks like to know God and live in his kingdom. He has continued to welcome the needy and challenge the religious authorities.

Now Jesus begins his journey to Jerusalem, where he knows his journey will come to an end. Shortly before entering Jerusalem, he passes through the city of Jericho.

READ LUKE 18:35-43

By now, Jesus' reputation has grown. Crowds gather to hear his teaching and see his miracles. Jesus is the topic of conversation and gossip. Even a blind beggar has heard of him.

Then the beggar discovers that, remarkably, Jesus is walking right past.

2.   **Why do you think those leading the crowd want to stop the beggar getting Jesus' attention?**

3.   **Why do you think the beggar is willing to ignore the opposition he faces?**

This man is blind, but he sees Jesus clearly. 'Son of David' is another name for the promised Messiah who would bring sight to the blind (see Luke 4:18–19).

The beggar knows that he does not have the power to change his situation, but he cries out, hoping that Jesus does. His hope proves to be well placed. In kindness, Jesus gives him his sight.

4.   **Jesus honours the blind beggar for his 'faith'. What does this encounter reveal about what faith is?**

A blind beggar receives his sight

³⁵ As Jesus approached Jericho, a blind man was sitting by the roadside begging. ³⁶ When he heard the crowd going by, he asked what was happening. ³⁷ They told him, 'Jesus of Nazareth is passing by.'

³⁸ He called out, 'Jesus, Son of David, have mercy on me!'

³⁹ Those who led the way rebuked him and told him to be quiet, but he shouted all the more, 'Son of David, have mercy on me!'

⁴⁰ Jesus stopped and ordered the man to be brought to him. When he came near, Jesus asked him, ⁴¹ 'What do you want me to do for you?'

'Lord, I want to see,' he replied.

⁴² Jesus said to him, 'Receive your sight; your faith has healed you.' ⁴³ Immediately he received his sight and followed Jesus, praising God. When all the people saw it, they also praised God.

The man follows Jesus into the city of Jericho, where another man is waiting to see Jesus.

READ LUKE 19:1-7

Tax collectors were Judeans who were responsible for taking Roman taxes from their fellow people. They had a reputation for being abusive and corrupt. Zacchaeus is a 'chief tax collector', likely a manager in this exploitative system.

Like the beggar, Zacchaeus has heard of Jesus. And he wants to see what he is like.

5. **In Zacchaeus' culture, running and climbing trees were undignified things for an adult to do. Why do you think Zacchaeus acts in this way?**

Surrounded by a crowd, Jesus reaches the tree that Zacchaeus is sitting in. He stops. He looks up.

6. **How do you think Zacchaeus is feeling as Jesus' eyes fix on him? What might he and the crowd have been expecting Jesus to do?**

Jesus inviting himself to Zacchaeus' house is a sign of respect and friendship. The crowd grumbles about Jesus relating to Zacchaeus in this way.

7. **Why do you think Jesus is willing to identify himself with a man like Zacchaeus?**

8. **Imagine you are Zacchaeus. As you walk with Jesus and enjoy a meal with him, how do you think you would be feeling?**

Zacchaeus the tax collector

19 Jesus entered Jericho and was passing through. ² A man was there by the name of Zacchaeus; he was a chief tax collector and was wealthy. ³ He wanted to see who Jesus was, but because he was short he could not see over the crowd. ⁴ So he ran ahead and climbed a sycamore-fig tree to see him, since Jesus was coming that way. ⁵ When Jesus reached the spot, he looked up and said to him, 'Zacchaeus, come down immediately. I must stay at your house today.' ⁶ So he came down at once and welcomed him gladly.

⁷ All the people saw this and began to mutter, 'He has gone to be the guest of a sinner.'

As an expression of turning from his old life and turning to Jesus, Zacchaeus gives away most of his possessions.

9. **Why do you think Zacchaeus feels able to change his life in such a costly way?**

Jesus willingly experiences the hostility of the crowd to welcome Zacchaeus. And Zacchaeus is changed. Not by anything from within him, but because of Jesus and his kindness.

Jesus describes what has happened to Zacchaeus as 'salvation'. He is now a 'son of Abraham', he is part of God's family. He was lost, but now he is found.

10. **On the surface, Zacchaeus and the blind beggar are very different, but what do they have in common?**

We might see the beggar as an oppressed sufferer and Zacchaeus as a corrupt oppressor. But both face obstacles they cannot overcome by themselves. Both reach out to Jesus. Both receive his kindness. Both are transformed.

Yet Jesus' words in verse 10 suggest there is something more going on. It is not just that these men were seeking Jesus. Could it be that, all along, he was seeking them?

11. **Jesus says that he has come to 'seek and to save the lost.' Considering his interactions with these two men, what do you think that means?**

⁸ But Zacchaeus stood up and said to the Lord, 'Look, Lord! Here and now I give half of my possessions to the poor, and if I have cheated anybody out of anything, I will pay back four times the amount.'

⁹ Jesus said to him, 'Today salvation has come to this house, because this man, too, is a son of Abraham. ¹⁰ For the Son of Man came to seek and to save the lost.'

Process **together**

Everything about the transformation these men experience is down to Jesus and his love.

It means that their transformation is more than mere self-improvement. These men discover that their life is no longer about them, but about Jesus. The beggar follows Jesus down the road into a new adventure. Zacchaeus gives up his wealth, called into a life of costly generosity.

Today, Jesus calls people in a similar way: into a life of new horizons, new joys, and new costs.

12. **What would you need to know about Jesus to trust him to transform you in this way?**

These men were lost and alienated – from others, but ultimately from God. The same is true for us. Jesus' purpose is to call us into a relationship with God. As he seeks people like us, he invites us into a life of greater joy and purpose.

13. **Is there anything in your life that makes you think that Jesus might be seeking you?**

The parable of the ten minas

[11] While they were listening to this, he went on to tell them a parable, because he was near Jerusalem and the people thought that the kingdom of God was going to appear at once. [12] He said: 'A man of noble birth went to a distant country to have himself appointed king and then to return. [13] So he called ten of his servants and gave them ten minas. "Put this money to work," he said, "until I come back."

[14] 'But his subjects hated him and sent a delegation after him to say, "We don't want this man to be our king."

[15] 'He was made king, however, and returned home. Then he sent for the servants to whom he had given the money, in order to find out what they had gained with it.

[16] 'The first one came and said, "Sir, your mina has earned ten more."

[17] "Well done, my good servant!" his master replied. "Because you have been trustworthy in a very small matter, take charge of ten cities."

[18] 'The second came and said, "Sir, your mina has earned five more."

[19] 'His master answered, "You take charge of five cities."

[20] 'Then another servant came and said, "Sir, here is your mina; I have kept it laid away in a piece of cloth. [21] I was afraid of you, because you are a hard man. You take out what you did not put in and reap what you did not sow."

[22] 'His master replied, "I will judge you by your own words, you wicked servant! You knew, did you, that I am a hard man, taking out what I did not put in, and reaping what I did not sow? [23] Why then didn't you put my money on deposit, so that when I came back, I could have collected it with interest?"

[24] 'Then he said to those standing by, "Take his mina away from him and give it to the one who has ten minas."

25 "Sir," they said, 'he already has ten!'

26 'He replied, "I tell you that to everyone who has, more will be given, but as for the one who has nothing, even what they have will be taken away. 27 But those enemies of mine who did not want me to be king over them - bring them here and kill them in front of me."

Jesus comes to Jerusalem as king

28 After Jesus had said this, he went on ahead, going up to Jerusalem. 29 As he approached Bethphage and Bethany at the hill called the Mount of Olives, he sent two of his disciples, saying to them, 30 'Go to the village ahead of you, and as you enter it, you will find a colt tied there, which no one has ever ridden. Untie it and bring it here. 31 If anyone asks you, "Why are you untying it?" say, "The Lord needs it."

32 Those who were sent ahead went and found it just as he had told them. 33 As they were untying the colt, its owners asked them, 'Why are you untying the colt?'

34 They replied, 'The Lord needs it.'

35 They brought it to Jesus, threw their cloaks on the colt and put Jesus on it. 36 As he went along, people spread their cloaks on the road.

37 When he came near the place where the road goes down the Mount of Olives, the whole crowd of disciples began joyfully to praise God in loud voices for all the miracles they had seen:

38 'Blessed is the king who comes in the name of the Lord!'
'Peace in heaven and glory in the highest!'

39 Some of the Pharisees in the crowd said to Jesus, 'Teacher, rebuke your disciples!'

40 'I tell you,' he replied, 'if they keep quiet, the stones will cry out.'

41 As he approached Jerusalem and saw the city, he wept over it

⁴² and said, 'If you, even you, had only known on this day what would bring you peace - but now it is hidden from your eyes. ⁴³ The days will come upon you when your enemies will build an embankment against you and encircle you and hem you in on every side. ⁴⁴ They will dash you to the ground, you and the children within your walls. They will not leave one stone on another, because you did not recognise the time of God's coming to you.'

Jesus at the temple

⁴⁵ When Jesus entered the temple courts, he began to drive out those who were selling. ⁴⁶ 'It is written,' he said to them, "My house will be a house of prayer"; but you have made it "a den of robbers."

⁴⁷ Every day he was teaching at the temple. But the chief priests, the teachers of the law and the leaders among the people were trying to kill him. ⁴⁸ Yet they could not find any way to do it, because all the people hung on his words.

The authority of Jesus questioned

20 One day as Jesus was teaching the people in the temple courts and proclaiming the good news, the chief priests and the teachers of the law, together with the elders, came up to him. ² 'Tell us by what authority you are doing these things,' they said. 'Who gave you this authority?'

³ He replied, 'I will also ask you a question. Tell me: ⁴ John's baptism - was it from heaven, or of human origin?'

⁵ They discussed it among themselves and said, 'If we say, "From heaven," he will ask, "Why didn't you believe him?" ⁶ But if we say, "Of human origin," all the people will stone us, because they are persuaded that John was a prophet.'

⁷ So they answered, 'We don't know where it was from.'

⁸ Jesus said, 'Neither will I tell you by what authority I am doing these things.'

The parable of the tenants

⁹ He went on to tell the people this parable: 'A man planted a vineyard, rented it to some farmers and went away for a long time. ¹⁰ At harvest time he sent a servant to the tenants so they would give him some of the fruit of the vineyard. But the tenants beat him and sent him away empty-handed. ¹¹ He sent another servant, but that one also they beat and treated shamefully and sent away empty-handed. ¹² He sent still a third, and they wounded him and threw him out.

¹³ '"Then the owner of the vineyard said, "What shall I do? I will send my son, whom I love; perhaps they will respect him."

¹⁴ 'But when the tenants saw him, they talked the matter over. "This is the heir," they said. "Let's kill him, and the inheritance will be ours."

¹⁵ So they threw him out of the vineyard and killed him.

'What then will the owner of the vineyard do to them? ¹⁶ He will come and kill those tenants and give the vineyard to others.'

When the people heard this, they said, 'God forbid!'

¹⁷ Jesus looked directly at them and asked, 'Then what is the meaning of that which is written:

"The stone the builders rejected
   has become the cornerstone"?

¹⁸ Everyone who falls on that stone will be broken to pieces; anyone on whom it falls will be crushed.'

¹⁹ The teachers of the law and the chief priests looked for a way to arrest him immediately, because they knew he had spoken this parable against them. But they were afraid of the people.

Paying taxes to Caesar

²⁰ Keeping a close watch on him, they sent spies, who pretended to be sincere. They hoped to catch Jesus in something he said, so

that they might hand him over to the power and authority of the governor. ²¹ So the spies questioned him: 'Teacher, we know that you speak and teach what is right, and that you do not show partiality but teach the way of God in accordance with the truth. ²² Is it right for us to pay taxes to Caesar or not?'

²³ He saw through their duplicity and said to them, ²⁴ 'Show me a denarius. Whose image and inscription are on it?'

'Caesar's,' they replied.

²⁵ He said to them, 'Then give back to Caesar what is Caesar's, and to God what is God's.'

²⁶ They were unable to trap him in what he had said there in public. And astonished by his answer, they became silent.

The resurrection and marriage

²⁷ Some of the Sadducees, who say there is no resurrection, came to Jesus with a question. ²⁸ 'Teacher,' they said, 'Moses wrote for us that if a man's brother dies and leaves a wife but no children, the man must marry the widow and raise up offspring for his brother. ²⁹ Now there were seven brothers. The first one married a woman and died childless. ³⁰ The second ³¹ and then the third married her, and in the same way the seven died, leaving no children. ³² Finally, the woman died too. ³³ Now then, at the resurrection whose wife will she be, since the seven were married to her?'

³⁴ Jesus replied, 'The people of this age marry and are given in marriage. ³⁵ But those who are considered worthy of taking part in the age to come and in the resurrection from the dead will neither marry nor be given in marriage, ³⁶ and they can no longer die; for they are like the angels. They are God's children, since they are children of the resurrection. ³⁷ But in the account of the burning bush, even Moses showed that the dead rise, for he calls the Lord 'the God of Abraham, and the God of Isaac, and the God of Jacob.'

³⁸ He is not the God of the dead, but of the living, for to him all are alive.'

³⁹ Some of the teachers of the law responded, 'Well said, teacher!' ⁴⁰ And no one dared to ask him any more questions.

Whose son is the Messiah?

⁴¹ Then Jesus said to them, 'Why is it said that the Messiah is the son of David? ⁴² David himself declares in the Book of Psalms:

> "'The Lord said to my Lord:
> 'Sit at my right hand
> ⁴³ until I make your enemies
> a footstool for your feet.'"

⁴⁴ David calls him "Lord." How then can he be his son?'

Warning against the teachers of the law

⁴⁵ While all the people were listening, Jesus said to his disciples,

⁴⁶ 'Beware of the teachers of the law. They like to walk around in flowing robes and love to be greeted with respect in the market-places and have the most important seats in the synagogues and the places of honour at banquets. ⁴⁷ They devour widows' houses and for a show make lengthy prayers. These men will be punished most severely.'

The widow's offering

21 As Jesus looked up, he saw the rich putting their gifts into the temple treasury. ² He also saw a poor widow put in two very small copper coins. ³ 'Truly I tell you,' he said, 'this poor widow has put in more than all the others. ⁴ All these people gave their gifts out of their wealth; but she out of her poverty put in all she had to live on.'

The destruction of the temple and signs of the end times

⁵ Some of his disciples were remarking about how the temple was adorned with beautiful stones and with gifts dedicated to God. But Jesus said, ⁶ 'As for what you see here, the time will come when not one stone will be left on another; every one of them will be thrown down.'

⁷ 'Teacher,' they asked, 'when will these things happen? And what will be the sign that they are about to take place?'

⁸ He replied: 'Watch out that you are not deceived. For many will come in my name, claiming, "I am he," and, "The time is near." Do not follow them. ⁹ When you hear of wars and uprisings, do not be frightened. These things must happen first, but the end will not come right away.'

¹⁰ Then he said to them: 'Nation will rise against nation, and kingdom against kingdom. ¹¹ There will be great earthquakes, famines and pestilences in various places, and fearful events and great signs from heaven.

¹² 'But before all this, they will seize you and persecute you. They will hand you over to synagogues and put you in prison, and you will be brought before kings and governors, and all on account of my name. ¹³ And so you will bear testimony to me. ¹⁴ But make up your mind not to worry beforehand how you will defend yourselves. ¹⁵ For I will give you words and wisdom that none of your adversaries will be able to resist or contradict. ¹⁶ You will be betrayed even by parents, brothers and sisters, relatives and friends, and they will put some of you to death. ¹⁷ Everyone will hate you because of me. ¹⁸ But not a hair of your head will perish. ¹⁹ Stand firm, and you will win life.

²⁰ 'When you see Jerusalem being surrounded by armies, you will know that its desolation is near. ²¹ Then let those who are in Judea flee to the mountains, let those in the city get out, and let those in the country not enter the city. ²² For this is the time of punishment in fulfilment of all that has been written. ²³ How dreadful it will be in

those days for pregnant women and nursing mothers! There will be great distress in the land and wrath against this people. ²⁴ They will fall by the sword and will be taken as prisoners to all the nations. Jerusalem will be trampled on by the Gentiles until the times of the Gentiles are fulfilled.

²⁵ 'There will be signs in the sun, moon and stars. On the earth, nations will be in anguish and perplexity at the roaring and tossing of the sea. ²⁶ People will faint from terror, apprehensive of what is coming on the world, for the heavenly bodies will be shaken. ²⁷ At that time they will see the Son of Man coming in a cloud with power and great glory. ²⁸ When these things begin to take place, stand up and lift up your heads, because your redemption is drawing near.'

²⁹ He told them this parable: 'Look at the fig tree and all the trees.

³⁰ When they sprout leaves, you can see for yourselves and know that summer is near. ³¹ Even so, when you see these things happening, you know that the kingdom of God is near.

³² 'Truly I tell you, this generation will certainly not pass away until all these things have happened. ³³ Heaven and earth will pass away, but my words will never pass away.

³⁴ 'Be careful, or your hearts will be weighed down with carousing, drunkenness and the anxieties of life, and that day will close on you suddenly like a trap. ³⁵ For it will come on all those who live on the face of the whole earth. ³⁶ Be always on the watch, and pray that you may be able to escape all that is about to happen, and that you may be able to stand before the Son of Man.'

³⁷ Each day Jesus was teaching at the temple, and each evening he went out to spend the night on the hill called the Mount of Olives, ³⁸ and all the people came early in the morning to hear him at the temple.

Judas agrees to betray Jesus

22 Now the Festival of Unleavened Bread, called the Passover, was approaching, ² and the chief priests and the teachers of the law were looking for some way to get rid of Jesus, for they were afraid of the people. ³ Then Satan entered Judas, called Iscariot, one of the Twelve. ⁴ And Judas went to the chief priests and the officers of the temple guard and discussed with them how he might betray Jesus. ⁵ They were delighted and agreed to give him money. ⁶ He consented, and watched for an opportunity to hand Jesus over to them when no crowd was present.

The Last Supper

⁷ Then came the day of Unleavened Bread on which the Passover lamb had to be sacrificed. ⁸ Jesus sent Peter and John, saying, 'Go and make preparations for us to eat the Passover.'

⁹ 'Where do you want us to prepare for it?' they asked.

¹⁰ He replied, 'As you enter the city, a man carrying a jar of water will meet you. Follow him to the house that he enters, ¹¹ and say to the owner of the house, "The Teacher asks: Where is the guest room, where I may eat the Passover with my disciples?" ¹² He will show you a large room upstairs, all furnished. Make preparations there.'

¹³ They left and found things just as Jesus had told them. So they prepared the Passover.

¹⁴ When the hour came, Jesus and his apostles reclined at the table. ¹⁵ And he said to them, 'I have eagerly desired to eat this Passover with you before I suffer. ¹⁶ For I tell you, I will not eat it again until it finds fulfilment in the kingdom of God.'

¹⁷ After taking the cup, he gave thanks and said, 'Take this and divide it among you. ¹⁸ For I tell you I will not drink again from the fruit of the vine until the kingdom of God comes.'

¹⁹ And he took bread, gave thanks and broke it, and gave it to them, saying, 'This is my body given for you; do this in remembrance of me.'

²⁰ In the same way, after the supper he took the cup, saying, 'This cup is the new covenant in my blood, which is poured out for you.

²¹ But the hand of him who is going to betray me is with mine on the table. ²² The Son of Man will go as it has been decreed. But woe to that man who betrays him!' ²³ They began to question among themselves which of them it might be who would do this.

²⁴ A dispute also arose among them as to which of them was considered to be greatest. ²⁵ Jesus said to them, 'The kings of the Gentiles lord it over them; and those who exercise authority over them call themselves Benefactors. ²⁶ But you are not to be like that. Instead, the greatest among you should be like the youngest, and the one who rules like the one who serves. ²⁷ For who is greater, the one who is at the table or the one who serves? Is it not the one who is at the table? But I am among you as one who serves. ²⁸ You are those who have stood by me in my trials. ²⁹ And I confer on you a kingdom, just as my Father conferred one on me, ³⁰ so that you may eat and drink at my table in my kingdom and sit on thrones, judging the twelve tribes of Israel.

³¹ 'Simon, Simon, Satan has asked to sift all of you as wheat. ³² But I have prayed for you, Simon, that your faith may not fail. And when you have turned back, strengthen your brothers.'

³³ But he replied, 'Lord, I am ready to go with you to prison and to death.'

³⁴ Jesus answered, 'I tell you, Peter, before the rooster crows today, you will deny three times that you know me.'

³⁵ Then Jesus asked them, 'When I sent you without purse, bag or sandals, did you lack anything?'

'Nothing,' they answered.

³⁶ He said to them, 'But now if you have a purse, take it, and also a bag; and if you don't have a sword, sell your cloak and buy one.

³⁷ It is written: 'And he was numbered with the transgressors'; and I tell you that this must be fulfilled in me. Yes, what is written about me

is reaching its fulfilment.'

³⁸ The disciples said, 'See, Lord, here are two swords.'

'That's enough!' he replied.

Jesus prays on the Mount of Olives

³⁹ Jesus went out as usual to the Mount of Olives, and his disciples followed him. ⁴⁰ On reaching the place, he said to them, 'Pray that you will not fall into temptation.' ⁴¹ He withdrew about a stone's throw beyond them, knelt down and prayed, ⁴² 'Father, if you are willing, take this cup from me; yet not my will, but yours be done.' ⁴³ An angel from heaven appeared to him and strengthened him. ⁴⁴ And being in anguish, he prayed more earnestly, and his sweat was like drops of blood falling to the ground.

⁴⁵ When he rose from prayer and went back to the disciples, he found them asleep, exhausted from sorrow. ⁴⁶ 'Why are you sleeping?' he asked them. 'Get up and pray so that you will not fall into temptation.'

Jesus arrested

⁴⁷ While he was still speaking a crowd came up, and the man who was called Judas, one of the Twelve, was leading them. He approached Jesus to kiss him, ⁴⁸ but Jesus asked him, 'Judas, are you betraying the Son of Man with a kiss?'

⁴⁹ When Jesus' followers saw what was going to happen, they said, 'Lord, should we strike with our swords?' ⁵⁰ And one of them struck the servant of the high priest, cutting off his right ear.

⁵¹ But Jesus answered, 'No more of this!' And he touched the man's ear and healed him.

⁵² Then Jesus said to the chief priests, the officers of the temple guard, and the elders, who had come for him, 'Am I leading a rebellion, that you have come with swords and clubs? ⁵³ Every day I was with you in the temple courts, and you did not lay a hand on me. But this is your hour - when darkness reigns.'

Peter disowns Jesus

⁵⁴ Then seizing him, they led him away and took him into the house of the high priest. Peter followed at a distance. ⁵⁵ And when some there had kindled a fire in the middle of the courtyard and had sat down together, Peter sat down with them. ⁵⁶ A servant-girl saw him seated there in the firelight. She looked closely at him and said, 'This man was with him.'

⁵⁷ But he denied it. 'Woman, I don't know him,' he said.

⁵⁸ A little later someone else saw him and said, 'You also are one of them.'

'Man, I am not!' Peter replied.

⁵⁹ About an hour later another asserted, 'Certainly this fellow was with him, for he is a Galilean.'

⁶⁰ Peter replied, 'Man, I don't know what you're talking about!' Just as he was speaking, the rooster crowed. ⁶¹ The Lord turned and looked straight at Peter. Then Peter remembered the word the Lord had spoken to him: 'Before the cock crows today, you will disown me three times.' ⁶² And he went outside and wept bitterly.

The guards mock Jesus

⁶³ The men who were guarding Jesus began mocking and beating him. ⁶⁴ They blindfolded him and demanded, 'Prophesy! Who hit you?' ⁶⁵ And they said many other insulting things to him.

Jesus before Pilate and Herod

⁶⁶ At daybreak the council of the elders of the people, both the chief priests and the teachers of the law, met together, and Jesus was led before them. ⁶⁷ 'If you are the Messiah,' they said, 'tell us.'

Jesus answered, 'If I tell you, you will not believe me, ⁶⁸ and if I asked you, you would not answer. ⁶⁹ But from now on, the Son of Man will be seated at the right hand of the mighty God.'

⁷⁰ They all asked, 'Are you then the Son of God?'

He replied, 'You say that I am.'

⁷¹ Then they said, 'Why do we need any more testimony? We have heard it from his own lips.'

23 Then the whole assembly rose and led him off to Pilate. ² And they began to accuse him, saying, 'We have found this man subverting our nation. He opposes payment of taxes to Caesar and claims to be Messiah, a king.'

³ So Pilate asked Jesus, 'Are you the king of the Jews?'

'You have said so,' Jesus replied. ⁴ Then Pilate announced to the chief priests and the crowd, 'I find no basis for a charge against this man.' ⁵ But they insisted, 'He stirs up the people all over Judea by his teaching. He started in Galilee and has come all the way here.'

⁶ On hearing this, Pilate asked if the man was a Galilean. ⁷ When he learned that Jesus was under Herod's jurisdiction, he sent him to Herod, who was also in Jerusalem at that time.

⁸ When Herod saw Jesus, he was greatly pleased, because for a long time he had been wanting to see him. From what he had heard about him, he hoped to see him perform a sign of some sort. ⁹ He plied him with many questions, but Jesus gave him no answer.

¹⁰ The chief priests and the teachers of the law were standing there, vehemently accusing him. ¹¹ Then Herod and his soldiers ridiculed and mocked him. Dressing him in an elegant robe, they sent him back to Pilate. ¹² That day Herod and Pilate became friends - before this they had been enemies.

PAUSE

Sit in stillness for a moment.

LOOK

Notice what stands out in the artwork.

READ

Read the passage slowly, once or twice.

REFLECT

Use the questions to guide your
thoughts and response.

¹³ Pilate called together the chief priests, the rulers and the people, ¹⁴ and said to them, 'You brought me this man as one who was inciting the people to rebellion. I have examined him in your presence and have found no basis for your charges against him. ¹⁵ Neither has Herod, for he sent him back to us; as you can see, he has done nothing to deserve death. ¹⁶ Therefore, I will punish him and then release him.'

¹⁸ But the whole crowd shouted, 'Away with this man! Release Barabbas to us!' ¹⁹ (Barabbas had been thrown into prison for an insurrection in the city, and for murder.)

²⁰ Wanting to release Jesus, Pilate appealed to them again.

²¹ But they kept shouting, 'Crucify him! Crucify him!'

²² For the third time he spoke to them: 'Why? What crime has this man committed? I have found in him no grounds for the death penalty. Therefore I will have him punished and then release him.'

²³ But with loud shouts they insistently demanded that he be crucified, and their shouts prevailed. ²⁴ So Pilate decided to grant their demand.

²⁵ He released the man who had been thrown into prison for insurrection and murder, the one they asked for, and surrendered Jesus to their will.

During the Jewish feast of Passover, it was the Roman custom to release a prisoner on death row.

Pilate suggests the release of Jesus.

The crowds scream for Barabbas' release instead.

They shout for Jesus to be crucified.

1. **What does Luke emphasise in his descriptions of Jesus and Barabbas?**

2. **How do you think Barabbas would have felt as he stood released from his chains, watching Jesus being led to his death?**

Christians throughout history have identified themselves with Barabbas. They know they deserve judgement. They know that Jesus is perfectly innocent. And yet Jesus steps in to be judged in their place.

3. **How easy do you find it to relate to Barabbas?**

Look again at the artwork.
Does anything different stand out to you?

The crucifixion of Jesus

26 As the soldiers led him away, they seized Simon from Cyrene, who was on his way in from the country, and put the cross on him and made him carry it behind Jesus. 27 A large number of people followed him, including women who mourned and wailed for him. 28 Jesus turned and said to them, 'Daughters of Jerusalem, do not weep for me; weep for yourselves and for your children. 29 For the

time will come when you will say, "Blessed are the childless women, the wombs that never bore and the breasts that never nursed!"

³⁰ Then

"'they will say to the mountains, 'Fall on us!'
    and to the hills, 'Cover us!'"

³¹ For if people do these things when the tree is green, what will happen when it is dry?'

Love

Study 5

LUKE 23:32-49

Loving someone can be the most powerful thing we experience in life. It can also be the most painful.

DISCUSS

1. What is the greatest expression of love that you have ever witnessed or experienced?

2. What does it say about humanity that love can be so painful?

A lot has happened in the previous chapters. The religious leaders have become increasingly hostile to Jesus as he has exposed their hypocrisy and challenged their authority. They are outraged at Jesus' claim to be the promised Messiah of God.

As Jesus enters Jerusalem, their opposition reaches its violent conclusion. Although Jesus is totally innocent, he is betrayed by a friend and arrested. He faces an unjust trial, and is then beaten, humiliated, and sentenced to death.

Yet Jesus has repeatedly said that he must go to Jerusalem. He knew what was coming. He had even told his disciples what to expect on several occasions. Jesus is not a helpless victim: his death is something he is purposely choosing to suffer. We pick up the story as Jesus is led outside of the city walls to be killed.

READ LUKE 23:32-39

Crucifixion was a brutal and humiliating death. In Jewish understanding, to be crucified was a sign of being abandoned by God. The victim was stripped and nailed by their wrists and ankles to wooden beams. Luke describes the event in a simple phrase: 'they crucified him there'.

Luke is more interested in recording the words and actions of Jesus and those watching on. He wants his readers to understand the meaning behind it all.

3. **What words would you use to describe the way Jesus is treated as he is crucified?**

4. **As you read Jesus' words in verse 34, what are you left thinking and feeling?**

5. **Why do you think the rulers, soldiers, and criminal mock him in the way they do?**

³² Two other men, both criminals, were also led out with him to be executed. ³³ When they came to the place called the Skull, they crucified him there, along with the criminals - one on his right, the other on his left. ³⁴ Jesus said, 'Father, forgive them, for they do not know what they are doing.' And they divided up his clothes by casting lots.

³⁵ The people stood watching, and the rulers even sneered at him. They said, 'He saved others; let him save himself if he is God's Messiah, the Chosen One.'

³⁶ The soldiers also came up and mocked him. They offered him wine vinegar ³⁷ and said, 'If you are the king of the Jews, save yourself.'

³⁸ There was a written notice above him, which read: THIS IS THE KING OF THE JEWS.

³⁹ One of the criminals who hung there hurled insults at him: 'Aren't you the Messiah? Save yourself and us!'

The Skull - another name for a hill called Golgotha.
King of the Jews - a name for the Messiah, perhaps mockingly given to Jesus.

Though he had claimed to be the powerful Messiah king, Jesus is now ridiculed and defeated. But Luke draws our attention to another voice: the voice of another criminal crucified alongside Jesus.

READ LUKE 23:40-43

6. **What do the criminal's words reveal about his view of himself and his view of Jesus?**

7. **How do you think this criminal would have felt as he heard Jesus' promise?**

Luke is building a picture. Though Jesus is innocent, he is disgraced and about to die. Yet in love he looks to others. His words to the criminal whisper the possibility of forgiveness and life beyond death.

⁴⁰ But the other criminal rebuked him. 'Don't you fear God,' he said, 'since you are under the same sentence? ⁴¹ We are punished justly, for we are getting what our deeds deserve. But this man has done nothing wrong.' ⁴² Then he said, 'Jesus, remember me when you come into your kingdom.' ⁴³ Jesus answered him, 'Truly I tell you, today you will be with me in paradise.'

Suddenly, Luke zooms out. He describes two supernatural occurrences which display the cosmic significance of Jesus' death.

READ LUKE 23:44-49

The first supernatural occurrence is that darkness covers the entire land.

8.   **What do you think this darkness communicates about Jesus' crucifixion?**

For the Jewish people gathered to watch the crucifixion, their culture associated darkness with God's judgement.

The second supernatural occurrence is the ripping of the temple curtain. The curtain referred to is likely the huge curtain which separated the 'most holy place' from the rest of the temple. The 'most holy place' was where God symbolically dwelt, separated from human uncleanness and sin.

9.   **What does the tearing of this curtain suggest is happening as Jesus dies?**

The death of Jesus

⁴⁴ It was now about noon, and darkness came over the whole land until three in the afternoon, ⁴⁵ for the sun stopped shining. And the curtain of the temple was torn in two. ⁴⁶ Jesus called out with a loud voice, 'Father, into your hands I commit my spirit.' When he had said this, he breathed his last.

⁴⁷ The centurion, seeing what had happened, praised God and said, 'Surely this was a righteous man.' ⁴⁸ When all the people who had gathered to witness this sight saw what took place, they beat their breasts and went away. ⁴⁹ But all those who knew him, including the women who had followed him from Galilee, stood at a distance, watching these things.

Jesus has already given clues as to what will happen when he dies.

In Luke 22:37 Jesus said that he will be 'numbered with the transgressors'. He is quoting from a passage written by the prophet Isaiah. It describes the Messiah who would restore and heal God's people. Jesus says that he is that figure. Here is more of what Isaiah writes:

3 He was despised and rejected—
   a man of sorrows, acquainted with deepest grief.
We turned our backs on him and looked the other way...
5 ...But he was pierced for our rebellion, crushed for our sins.
He was beaten so we could be whole.
   He was whipped so we could be healed.
6 All of us, like sheep, have strayed away.
   We have left God's paths to follow our own.
Yet the Lord laid on him the sins of us all.
7 He was oppressed and treated harshly,
   yet he never said a word...
8 ...Unjustly condemned, he was led away.

Isaiah 53

(NLT)

10. Where do you see parallels between Isaiah's words and Jesus' death?

11. How do Isaiah's words help us to understand why Jesus died?

Process **together**

Luke has revealed the problem that lurks inside each of us: like the lost son, we have run away from the God who made us. Like Zacchaeus, we have lived for ourselves and harmed others. Like the religious rulers, we would rather push God to the side than have him interfere with our lives.

Each of us deserves to face God's anger and justice for how we have treated him. Yet in love, Jesus chooses to face that anger and justice in our place. The same offer extended to the criminal is extended to us. As he hangs above the crowd, Jesus offers each of us forgiveness, eternal life, and access to God.

12. **What does Jesus' death tell you about what humanity is like? What does it tell you about what Jesus is like?**

13. **How do you respond to Jesus' offer of forgiveness?**

PERSONAL
REFLECTION

PAUSE
Sit in stillness for a moment.

LOOK
Notice what stands out in the artwork.

READ
Read the passage slowly, once or twice.

REFLECT
Use the questions to guide your
thoughts and response.

The burial of Jesus

[50] Now there was a man named Joseph, a member of the Council, a good and upright man, [51] who had not consented to their decision and action. He came from the Judean town of Arimathea, and he himself was waiting for the kingdom of God. [52] Going to Pilate, he asked for Jesus' body. [53] Then he took it down, wrapped it in linen cloth and placed it in a tomb cut in the rock, one in which no one had yet been laid. [54] It was Preparation Day, and the Sabbath was about to begin.

[55] The women who had come with Jesus from Galilee followed Joseph and saw the tomb and how his body was laid in it. [56] Then they went home and prepared spices and perfumes. But they rested on the Sabbath in obedience to the commandment.

Jesus' reputation has been growing as he continued to speak and act with power and authority.

Jesus' followers were increasingly hopeful that he was going to bring about a better future.

But now, they find themselves preparing his body for burial. Death has robbed them of their hope.

1. **What do you imagine these followers now think of Jesus?**

2. **What questions might they have been left with?**

3. **As you have read Luke's Gospel, what questions remain unanswered for you?**

Look again at the artwork.
Does anything different stand out to you?

Trust

Study 6

LUKE 24:1-12 & 36-53

Trust does not come easily, especially if we have been let down before. But staying guarded, although it can feel safe, can also be exhausting.

1. What helps you to trust someone or something?

2. How easy do you find the process of trusting?

Jesus' death had shaken the trust his followers had in him. How could this happen to the Messiah? What hope of a rescue do they have now? What would happen to them?

Jesus' followers are scared and so hide. Apart from the women. Having seen him die, now they go to prepare his body with spices.

READ LUKE 24:1-3

2. **What questions might these women have as they arrive to find an empty tomb?**

READ LUKE 24:4-12

Two angels visit and remind the women of what Jesus had said about his death and what would follow. It is only then they realise what has happened: Jesus is alive. Their trust in him is restored.

However, as they share the news, the disciples remain sceptical.

3. **To what extent do you sympathise with the disciples' responses?**

4. **What do you think causes Peter to run off and look at the tomb for himself?**

5. **The linen cloths that Peter sees in the tomb were used to wrap Jesus' dead body. Why do you think they leave him 'wondering to himself'?**

Study continues on page 160

Jesus has risen

24 On the first day of the week, very early in the morning, the women took the spices they had prepared and went to the tomb. ² They found the stone rolled away from the tomb, ³ but when they entered, they did not find the body of the Lord Jesus.

⁴ While they were wondering about this, suddenly two men in clothes that gleamed like lightning stood beside them. ⁵ In their fright the women bowed down with their faces to the ground, but the men said to them, 'Why do you look for the living among the dead? ⁶ He is not here; he has risen! Remember how he told you, while he was still with you in Galilee: ⁷ "The Son of Man must be delivered over to the hands of sinners, be crucified and on the third day be raised again."'⁸ Then they remembered his words.

⁹ When they came back from the tomb, they told all these things to the Eleven and to all the others. ¹⁰ It was Mary Magdalene, Joanna, Mary the mother of James, and the others with them who told this to the apostles. ¹¹ But they did not believe the women, because their words seemed to them like nonsense. ¹² Peter, however, got up and ran to the tomb. Bending over, he saw the strips of linen lying by themselves, and he went away, wondering to himself what had happened.

Spices - fragrances used in the burying of dead bodies.

On the road to Emmaus

¹³ Now that same day two of them were going to a village called Emmaus, about seven miles from Jerusalem. ¹⁴ They were talking with each other about everything that had happened. ¹⁵ As they talked and discussed these things with each other, Jesus himself came up and walked along with them; ¹⁶ but they were kept from recognising him.

¹⁷ He asked them, 'What are you discussing together as you walk along?'

They stood still, their faces downcast. ¹⁸ One of them, named Cleopas, asked him, 'Are you the only one visiting Jerusalem who does not know the things that have happened there in these days?'

¹⁹ 'What things?' he asked.

'About Jesus of Nazareth,' they replied. 'He was a prophet, powerful in word and deed before God and all the people. ²⁰ The chief priests and our rulers handed him over to be sentenced to death, and they crucified him; ²¹ but we had hoped that he was the one who was going to redeem Israel. And what is more, it is the third day since all this took place. ²² In addition, some of our women amazed us. They went to the tomb early this morning ²³ but didn't find his body. They came and told us that they had seen a vision of angels, who said he was alive. ²⁴ Then some of our companions went to the tomb and found it just as the women had said, but they did not see Jesus.'

25 He said to them, 'How foolish you are, and how slow to believe all that the prophets have spoken! 26 Did not the Messiah have to suffer these things and then enter his glory?' 27 And beginning with Moses and all the Prophets, he explained to them what was said in all the Scriptures concerning himself.

28 As they approached the village to which they were going, Jesus continued on as if he were going further. 29 But they urged him strongly, 'Stay with us, for it is nearly evening; the day is almost over.' So he went in to stay with them.

30 When he was at the table with them, he took bread, gave thanks, broke it and began to give it to them. 31 Then their eyes were opened and they recognised him, and he disappeared from their sight.

32 They asked each other, 'Were not our hearts burning within us while he talked with us on the road and opened the Scriptures to us?'

33 They got up and returned at once to Jerusalem. There they found the Eleven and those with them, assembled together 34 and saying, 'It is true! The Lord has risen and has appeared to Simon.'

35 Then the two told what had happened on the way, and how Jesus was recognised by them when he broke the bread.

READ LUKE 24:36-43

We find the disciples hidden away, exchanging reports of what they have witnessed. The idea that Jesus had risen from the dead was as unbelievable to them as it us for us today. Dead people stay dead!

But an increasing number of people are reporting sightings. In verses 13 - 35, Jesus appears to two followers and separately to Peter. Along with the women they too are saying that Jesus is alive. But the rest of the disciples struggle to trust what they hear.

6. **Jesus' disciples first think he is a ghost. What does this show us about their expectations?**

7. **Why do you think Jesus speaks and acts in the way he does? What does he want the disciples to realise?**

Jesus appears to the disciples

36 While they were still talking about this, Jesus himself stood among them and said to them, 'Peace be with you.'

37 They were startled and frightened, thinking they saw a ghost. 38 He said to them, 'Why are you troubled, and why do doubts rise in your minds? 39 Look at my hands and my feet. It is I myself! Touch me and see; a ghost does not have flesh and bones, as you see I have.'

40 When he had said this, he showed them his hands and feet. 41 And while they still did not believe it because of joy and amazement, he asked them, 'Do you have anything here to eat?' 42 They gave him a piece of broiled fish, 43 and he took it and ate it in their presence.

Jesus gently helps the disciples to see that what seems too good to be true really has happened: he is alive and that changes everything.

8. **Imagine yourself as a disciple who has seen the resurrected Jesus. How might you be feeling now?**

9. **Having 'opened their minds', what does Jesus want the disciples to see?**

10. **Knowing that Jesus is risen from the dead, how do you think the disciples would have been transformed?**

The disciples' encounter with the risen Jesus was so undeniable that the most reasonable response was to trust him. Their disappointment was transformed to joy: a joy that caused them to go and share this hope with others, even though it led some to be imprisoned or killed.

11. **From what you have seen in Luke, what message of hope do these disciples now have to share?**

⁴⁴ He said to them, 'This is what I told you while I was still with you: Everything must be fulfilled that is written about me in the Law of Moses, the Prophets and the Psalms.'

⁴⁵ Then he opened their minds so they could understand the Scriptures. ⁴⁶ He told them, 'This is what is written: The Messiah will suffer and rise from the dead on the third day, ⁴⁷ and repentance for the forgiveness of sins will be preached in his name to all nations, beginning at Jerusalem. ⁴⁸ You are witnesses of these things. ⁴⁹ I am going to send you what my Father has promised; but stay in the city until you have been clothed with power from on high.'

The ascension of Jesus

⁵⁰ When he had led them out to the vicinity of Bethany, he lifted up his hands and blessed them. ⁵¹ While he was blessing them, he left them and was taken up into heaven. ⁵² Then they worshipped him and returned to Jerusalem with great joy. ⁵³ And they stayed continually at the temple, praising God.

Power from on high - the time when the disciples are filled with God's presence, the Holy Spirit.

Process **together**

As we come to the end of Luke's account, we end where we began.

Unexpected people in expected places have had their eyes opened to see a bigger story. A story of hope and joy. A story centered on Jesus. He is the long-promised Messiah, come to bring about a different kind of world.

In Luke's account, we have witnessed glimmers of this world: a kingdom where the vulnerable are welcomed, where human pain and suffering matter, where life is restored, and people can be brought back to God.

What was hinted at in the opening pages of Luke is now fully visible: the resurrected Jesus shows he really is the saviour that people were hoping for.

12.   How has your view of Jesus changed as you have read Luke's Gospel?

13.   What, if anything, keeps you from coming to Jesus to experience the hope and joy he promises?

Throughout his gospel, Luke has encouraged us to come to Jesus as needy people, to come with empty hands to receive his compassion and forgiveness. Like the disciples, as we trust him, our lives will be transformed. We can find new joy and purpose as our lives are shaped by knowing a risen saviour.

Next **steps**

Having experienced Luke's account of Jesus' life, where do you find yourself now? Wherever you are at, it is worth thinking about how you might continue this journey.

The best way to keep uncovering the life that Jesus offers is alongside other people.

Join your university Christian Union

Experience a community of students who explore together what it means to live as followers of Jesus today.

Try church

For thousands of years, Christians from all walks of life have gathered to worship God through prayer, reading the Bible, singing, baptism and Communion. Come and experience it for yourself and meet people who have been transformed by Jesus.

Pray

You might be at a point where you do not know everything about Jesus, but you do know enough: enough that you think what Luke has written is true and that Jesus is trustworthy; enough that you want to follow him and receive the life with God that he offers.

A relationship with God begins like any other, with a conversation.

Here is a prayer that you might want to say with a friend or by yourself to begin that relationship.

Dear God,

I'm sorry that I've tried to live for myself.

I've wandered away from you.

I admit that I need your help.

Thank you that Jesus came for people who are needy like me.

Thank you that Jesus died so that I could be forgiven.

Thank you that because of him I can have a relationship with you.

Please fill me with your Holy Spirit and help me to live for you.

Amen

If you have prayed this prayer, tell someone else who follows Jesus. You are just embarking on the beautiful adventure of living life with God. He gives us other people to journey alongside and support us as we follow Him.

This resource is produced by UCCF: The Christian Unions. UCCF is made up of hundreds of university Christian Unions across Great Britain. We exist to give every student on campus an opportunity to hear about Jesus. This resource has been developed to help you engage with the narrative of Luke's Gospel.

To find our more about Christian Unions, visit **uccf.org.uk**

Contact

Blue Boar House
5 Blue Boar Street
Oxford OX1 4EE

01865253678
info@uccf.org.uk
www.uccf.org.uk

Registered Charity in England and Wales (306137) and Scotland
(SC038499)

Designed by Joe Cook - uncledesign.co.uk